"Dale grabs you on the first page and won't let you go. If you're about to go to college and you don't have the guts to read this book first, you deserve exactly what you end up with instead."

—Seth Godin, author of *Stop Stealing Dreams*

"The traditional path to getting an education and establishing your career has been disrupted. In this remarkable book, Dale shows exactly how to create your own educational experience and live life on your own terms."

—Dan Schawbel, bestselling author of *Me 2.0*
and founder of Millennial Branding

"The ROI on college has plummeted while alternative pathways have proliferated. For savvy 'hackademics,' as Dale calls them, there are better, faster, cheaper alternatives. Young people should build a plan for a cost-effective degree and/or follow Dale's advice to hack a better education."

—Tom Vander Ark, managing director of Learn Capital
and author of *Getting Smart: How Digital Learning Is Changing the World*

"The DIY education revolution is in full force. Before you spend another dollar on tuition, you owe it to yourself to read this book."

—Chris Guillebeau, author of *The $100 Startup*

"College students pay more than quadruple in real terms what their parents paid twenty-five years ago for a vague credential, grim job prospects, and a crippling amount of debt. With *Hacking Your Education* and the UnCollege movement, Dale Stephens makes a compelling case that talented and motivated people can avoid this never-never land and learn even more."

—Peter Thiel, entrepreneur, investor, philanthropist, and cofounder of PayPal

continued . . .

"This is the book colleges don't want you to read. Because if more young people read this important book, the professors and college presidents would be out of jobs, but the students would get a much better education without all the debt and bullshit."

—Michael Ellsberg, author of *The Education of Millionaires*

"Brilliant and incredibly useful to anyone already doubting the school system but unsure of the alternate path. Dale's book is one step ahead, showing you great and practical examples of how to thrive without limits, without school."

—Derek Sivers, founder of CD Baby and author of *Anything You Want*

HACKING
YOUR
EDUCATION

Ditch the Lectures,
Save Tens of Thousands,
and Learn More Than Your Peers Ever Will

DALE J. STEPHENS

A PERIGEE BOOK

A PERIGEE BOOK
Published by the Penguin Group
Penguin Group (USA) Inc.
375 Hudson Street, New York, New York 10014, USA

USA / Canada / UK / Ireland / Australia / New Zealand / India / South Africa / China

Penguin Books Ltd., Registered Offices: 80 Strand, London WC2R 0RL, England
For more information about the Penguin Group, visit penguin.com

First edition: March 2013

Library of Congress Cataloging-in-Publication Data

Stephens, Dale J.
Hacking your education : ditch the lectures, save tens of thousands, and
learn more than your peers ever will / Dale J. Stephens.
p.   cm.
Includes bibliographical references.
ISBN 978-0-399-15996-1
1. Self-culture.   2. Education, Higher.   I. Title.
LC32.S74   2013
371.39'43—dc23   2012045086

PRINTED IN THE UNITED STATES OF AMERICA

10 9 8 7 6 5 4 3 2 1

Text design by Kristin del Rosario

While the author has made every effort to provide accurate telephone numbers, Internet addresses, and
other contact information at the time of publication, neither the publisher nor the author assumes any
responsibility for errors, or for changes that occur after publication. Further, the publisher does not have
any control over and does not assume any responsibility for author or third-party websites or their content.

Most Perigee books are available at special quantity discounts for bulk purchases for sales promotions,
premiums, fund-raising, or educational use. Special books, or book excerpts, can also be created
to fit specific needs. For details, write: Special Markets, Penguin Group (USA) Inc.,
375 Hudson Street, New York, New York 10014.

CONTENTS

For my parents.
Thank for your love and the freedom you gave me.

ABOUT UNCOLLEGE.ORG

UnCollege.org offers self-directed learners resources to help hack their education in the form of online content and real-world educational experiences. Hackademics Camps offer a deep dive into self-directed learning. In 2013, the UnCollege Gap Year program will launch, offering an exclusive group of ten young people the opportunity to explore self-directed learning for a year instead of going to college. To apply, visit www.uncollege.org/gapyear.

INTRODUCTION

You wasted $150,000 on an education
for $1.50 in late fees at the public library?
—MATT DAMON IN *GOOD WILL HUNTING*

"SO, WHERE DO YOU GO TO SCHOOL?"

I turned to the speaker, a motherly looking woman in her midforties. We were at a cocktail party at a hip bar in Palo Alto, the center of Silicon Valley, so she expected me to say Stanford, the university just a mile away. Instead, I said: "I don't. I dropped out of elementary school. And I dropped out of college."

Her eyes widened. "What do you do instead? Where do you live? How do you support yourself?"

Before I could answer any of these questions, she stopped, looked at me very seriously, and asked, "Do you have a girlfriend?"

Was there something very obvious that I wasn't understanding? Is the purpose of college really as straightforward as finding a girlfriend (or in my case, a boyfriend)? If that's the case, I've been totally wasting my time.

The question of where you went to school is one everyone gets asked. We ask because we assume that school is a positive experience and a formative part of our lives. But maybe we're asking the wrong thing. After all, this woman didn't really care where I went to college. If I'd said Stanford, she would have nodded, smiled, and moved on to an equally superficial question like "Where do you live?" This question-and-answer game reflects a malady of society: university descriptions as self-descriptions.

Perhaps what we should be asking at cocktail parties is not, Where do you go to school? but, Why did you go to school? Answering that question requires some thought. And you might not know the answer. There's nothing wrong with going to school, but if you attend a university, you should know exactly why you're doing it.

My own path to this point had been circuitous, to say the least. I dropped out of school after fifth grade. I hadn't received any formal education for more than six years. Instead of sitting in class in high school, copying notes from a blackboard, I'd spent the last six years working on political campaigns, living in France, and starting my own businesses. And yet here I was at a university. Despite years of experience to the contrary, I still felt that all roads led to an ivy-covered institution.

Going to college is meant to be the culmination of twelve years of hard work, determination, and study. You're told that if you get good grades, ace the SAT, and do lots of extracurriculars, you'll get into a good university. The reasoning seems solid when you're in high school—after all, everyone tells you that college graduates earn more and are less likely to be unemployed.

I enrolled in Hendrix College, an elite private liberal arts college, with high hopes. Any idealism I had about university was quickly squashed. For the most part, people weren't there to learn; they were there to party for four years and, if they rolled into class without a hangover, to learn something along the way. I soon started asking questions. If the best experiences happen outside the classroom, why am I paying $42,000 a year to sit *inside* a classroom? A fifty-minute class costs you about $250, given the average cost of tuition. Are most classes worth that? What else could you accomplish every hour with that time and money? Is it really worth going into an average of $27,000 in debt just to get a degree? Will your degree even get you a job when 44.4 percent of college grads under twenty-five are unemployed or working jobs that don't require their degree?

After my first semester, I registered the domain UnCollege.org and began writing publicly about my frustrations at college. In March, I dropped out. I moved back to San Francisco, figuring I'd get a job. The company that I'd worked at before offered me a position. Great, I thought, life is settled. But when I got to San Francisco, it became clear that I wouldn't be taking that job. UnCollege was picking up steam, and I had work to do.

Part of that work turned into this book. This is *not* a book about dropping out but rather about becoming empowered to make your own decisions. I will teach you the steps required to hack your education. The chapters include suggested actions that you can take *right now* to start shaping your own education. We'll explore how school has failed almost everyone in some way and discuss the wrong and right reasons for going to college. I'll teach you the mind-set of the hackademic and how to identify your talents. I'll show you how to find mentors and how to build a network and create a community of people you love.

If you're looking for an easy solution, shortcut, or way to work less, this book is not for you. Hacking your education requires tons of hard work and determination. I'll share the stories of how people just like you kept themselves motivated, and how you can too.

You'll learn to grab your education by the horns, create opportunities for yourself, and change the world. If you're an eighteen-year-old freshman in college, this book will help you cultivate the skills and mind-set you need to thrive in the real world. If you're a twenty-six-year-old medical student, this book will help you think about your education in an entrepreneurial fashion and maximize the value of your experience.

CHAPTER ONE

Understanding the System

I WENT TO COLLEGE BECAUSE I ASSUMED I NEEDED A COLLEGE DEGREE to get a good job. When I realized that wasn't the case, I left. Thinking back on it now, I went to college because I wanted to do the things I believed only college graduates could do. Visions of handsome jobs, alumni networks, and all-night parties filled my teenage mind. What I realized is that the fantasy isn't the college degree. The fantasy is the path to success a college education is supposed to open. It turns out you can skip college entirely and learn more than your peers ever will.

We shouldn't be asking, How can I get a college degree? Instead, we should ask, How can I get the things a degree promises?

As I see it, there are three main reasons we go to university:

1. For the social experience

2. To get a job
3. To learn for learning's sake

The social life at college, we're told, is supposed to be the high point of our existence. We're supposed to stay up in our dorms having late-night conversations and making friends whom we'll know for the rest of our lives. We're supposed to join student groups, Greek organizations, and play in the marching band.

The promise is that getting a degree will help secure a job. In fact, we're told, it's nearly impossible to get a job without a degree. Even if college costs have skyrocketed over the last three decades, it's still worth the return on investment to spend tens of thousands of dollars and four years in college because you'll earn more over the rest of your lifetime, adults say. And if you look around, everyone is doing it. If all your friends are getting degrees, you better get one, too. You'd be stupid not to, right?

We expect our university professors to be wonderful wise sages who dispense knowledge daily. They're supposed to have a unique ability to synthesize and explain knowledge in lecture-size chunks. Don't worry about the major, the admission counselors say; take classes that interest you. After all, college is about getting a broad intellectual background and becoming an educated member of society.

Valid reasons? Sure. But if you take a step back, you have to wonder, do most universities deliver on these promises? Do I need to join student groups or could I move to a city and join interest-based groups there? Do I need a degree to get a job or could I teach myself to program computers? Do I need to listen to lectures or could I just go to the library and start reading?

I am, admittedly, a little biased in my assessment of these reasons to go to college. Again, they are all absolutely valid. The point I want to make is this: You, and you alone, must decide for yourself why you are in college. Take a moment to think about the question. Why are you in college? Are you in college because you want to enter a licensed profession, such as medicine? Are you in college because you like the structure that college provides? Are you in college because you got a huge scholarship?

Say you walk into a Starbucks. There's a long line, and everyone you know wants a cup of coffee. You're given a limited menu of choices—you've got coffee, mochas, and lattes in various flavors and styles. But maybe you think about it a minute and realize you don't really want *any* of those things. What then? The menu never says it, but you do have another choice—you can walk out. When you go to a university, you're given the choice between a limited set of paths. If you want to go to law school or med school, great! You've come to the right place. No one ever tells you, but you can instead make your own choice, and walk out.

Over the course of this book, I'm going to share with you the stories of people who made their own choices. Instead of taking predefined paths, they chose to create their own. Not all of them dropped out of a university. Some have degrees. Some never even went to college. But the common thread that holds them together is that they weren't afraid to create their own path.

Education is not a means to an end. It's not something you do for twelve years so you can get into a university, and then something you do for four more years so you can get a job sitting at a desk forty hours per week. Learning is a lifelong process. It happens all the time. It starts before we are born and continues until the day we die.

HOW COLLEGE REALLY IS

Aren't you going to miss the beer and girls at college?
—AN ACQUAINTANCE

"So what have you accomplished that you're most proud of?"

Had a hackademic been at that Palo Alto cocktail party, this is the question she would have asked. Hackademics want to know about what you've built, what you've created that has added value to the world, not how many letters you have after your name.

In this section, I'm going to challenge you to think like a hackademic by providing counterarguments for the three reasons for going to college: the social experience, the job opportunities, and the love of learning.

The Social Experience of College

A few days before I left college, I was having dinner in the cafeteria with friends who were asking me questions about leaving school. "Where will you live?" they asked, and "How will you support yourself?" These were serious questions, and I gave serious answers until a voice piped up at the end of the table.

"What about the beer and the girls?" a guy from my English class asked. "Aren't you going to miss them?"

I couldn't help but laugh. Not because drinking and having sex weren't priorities for me—they were and continue to be—but rather because he thought those were activities exclusive to the university. In my case, I figured I'd find more opportunities for both in San Francisco than I would at college in Arkansas. And in my case, I was right—my social life and sex life are far better now than they ever were in college.*

There are a lot of things that we assume exist only at universities but that in fact exist in the real world too. It's also wrong to assume that the only place to make lifelong friends is in college or the only place to join interest-based communities is in college or the only place to build a professional network is in college.

As an unschooler, I made friends because of interests and ideas, not just because I lived in the same dorm as someone else. I speak French and as an unschooler ran a French conversation group. When I moved back to California, I restarted this practice. I invited a few French speakers over and asked them to bring friends along. In doing so, I made friends based around a common interest.

In college, I joined the improv group, and when I moved back to San Francisco I at first wondered how I might find peers to continue doing improv with. Then I used Google to search for "San Francisco

---

* Mostly because (a) I prefer boys and champagne, and dating men wasn't so cool in Arkansas, and (b) Hendrix was in a dry county. Seriously. You had to drive twenty miles to buy booze.

improv" and turned up a dozen improv clubs in the city with drop-in workshops and classes. I began going to one on Tuesday evenings.

This book will teach you to think about your social experiences in different ways. Instead of haphazardly stumbling down your dorm hallway, you'll learn how to create intentional communities based on common values. You can do this both by hosting events, like a dinner party, or by organizing social gatherings, say an outing to a bowling club. You can also tap into existing communities using tools like Meetup (www.meetup.com) or local resources.

Going to College to Get a Job

> *School is the advertising agency which makes you*
> *believe that you need the society as it is.*
> —IVAN ILLICH

It's true that going to college for four years might get you a job. But that's hardly a guarantee today. A 2011 article in the *New York Times*, titled "Many with New College Degrees Find Job Market Humbling," covered graduates who can't find jobs, reporting that 22.4 percent of college grads under twenty-five are unemployed and another 22 percent are working jobs that don't require a college degree.[1] The scene is no brighter for those with terminal degrees. In fall 2010, the *Chronicle of Higher Education* found that there were fifty-seven hundred janitors in the United States with PhDs.[2] I'm sure these are talented people—it's sad to see their brilliance go unused.

When I started writing this book in 2011, the average student graduated $25,000 or so in debt. By 2012, it was up to $27,000 in debt. By the time you read this sentence, it will have increased another couple grand. Please, whatever you do, try not to take on student loans. Here's why:

1. When you graduate college with an average of $27,000 in debt, you're stuck in a narrow track, needing to find a job to pay off the debt. You are mortgaging away your freedom to innovate in exchange for a degree. Sure, there are people who owe much less than that but there are lots of people with lots *more* debt. It is a fucking terrible idea to start out your life with $27,000 hanging over your head.
2. Student loan debt is unforgivable in the case of bankruptcy. Yes, that's right. You can declare bankruptcy and not pay back your credit cards, and the bank can repossess your house, but you're stuck with loans until you're dead.

However, if you already have student loans, what is done is done. You have to live with reality, and you should start paying them off as quickly as possible. For a great perspective and ideas about how to go to school without going into debt, check out my friend Zac Bissonnette's book *Debt-Free U*. For inspiration and ideas for how to pay down your student debt, check out Joe Mihalic's blog *No More Harvard Debt* (www.nomoreharvarddebt.com). He graduated from Harvard Business School with $90,000 in debt, and he paid it all off in seven months. Or, instead of taking on debt, consider going to a university in Finland, where all higher education is free, even for international students.

If you want to be a doctor, medical school is a wise choice—I don't recommend keeping cadavers in your garage. However, for nonlicensed professions, college may no longer be a good investment. Since 1980, college tuition has risen more than 350 percent adjusted for inflation.[3] Yes, the College Board will point out that there is a wage premium for college graduates: Each year of college education leads to an 8 percent increase in overall lifetime earnings.[4] This is true today, but will it be true in the future? In 2010, student loan debt outpaced credit card debt and topped *$1 trillion* at the end of 2011.[5]

I Love to Learn, Therefore I Go to College

If college were teaching useful skills, 22.4 percent of college grads under age twenty-five wouldn't be unemployed. In their book *Academically Adrift*, Richard Arum, a sociologist at New York University, and Josipa Roska, a sociologist at the University of Virginia, demonstrated that undergraduate education is losing academic rigor.[6] Thirty-six percent of students showed no improvement in critical thinking, complex reasoning, or writing (as measured by the Collegiate Learning Assessment) over four years of college. According to the labor economists Philip S. Babcock and Mindy S. Marks, the average student spent only about fourteen hours per week studying in 2010—about half the amount a full-time college student studied in 1960.[7]

If you really wanted to learn, why not join your local library? The books are free, and you could invite your friends over and start an interest-based discussion group. You could even invite someone who is an expert on the subject you're discussing to give a short talk. It would be almost like college, except free and in the real world.

The point is, if you want to learn in college, you're going to have to fight. The odds are against you: The professors are researching, the students are partying, and the administrators are building new state-of-the-art gyms every few months. None of these people has a direct incentive to help you learn. The professors want to publish papers to get tenure. The students want to get a degree in the easiest way possible. The administrators are waiting for your tuition checks. But you have to recall: Universities do not exist to train you for the real world; they exist to make money. If you want to learn the skills required to navigate the world—the hustle, networking, and creativity—you're going to have to hack your own education. This book will teach you how to go deeper than college and learn in a lifelong way.

Why Hacking?

The systems and institutions that we see around us—of school, college, and work—are being systematically dismantled. We've seen a rise in the popularity of homeschooling and unschooling in the last ten years—from 1.1 million in 2003 to 1.5 million in 2007 in America.[8] The same is true of the breakdown of traditional work—freelancing is becoming more and more prevalent. But no one has told the story of what happens in between, when that sacred institution we call the university ceases to exist.

When I give people advice about their education, I focus on the importance of being a hackademic. When you're a hackademic, you're less interested in someone's résumé and more interested in her passions. You understand that institutions are malleable, and you bend those institutions to shape your own education and career. Most important, as a hackademic you know that you don't need to ask your parents, your teachers, your friends, or society for permission to build your future.

If you bought this book, chances are you don't want to sit in a classroom until you're twenty-two or older before being allowed to join the real world. Whether your dream is to travel, build a startup, make a difference, or just navigate a simple career change, these pages will show you how to do that here and now instead of after the often-elusive graduation. You can learn more than your peers ever will in four years.

Along my own way, I've met many amazing people who've also hacked their educations to wild success. These fellow hackademics made their way by identifying and honing their talents and building networks of peers and mentors. Now they're running multinational corporations, DJing at events around the world, and starting businesses. Not all of them dropped out of school, but all of them learned their most valuable lessons from real-life experiences, not classrooms. These are people who moved to Paris or became ship captains or created art instead of going to college.

You don't need to be a genius to take charge of your own education. What you do need is curiosity, determination, and a little grit. There is a theme of entrepreneurship throughout these pages. This is no accident. But that doesn't mean that you have to drop out of college and start a company! Even if you've never considered being an entrepreneur in the traditional sense, by the end of this book you'll be taking an entrepreneurial approach to your education.

WHAT YOU CAN DO INSTEAD OF COLLEGE

Have you ever seen the movie *Accepted*? My friend Rebecca Goldman first explained it to me like this: It's about a bunch of kids who are rejected from college and instead decide to start their own college. They commandeer an old school and create their own classes.

Like me, Rebecca is an unschooler. She never went to school before college. Instead, she was living in Kenya running marketing for a nongovernmental organization (NGO) or representing the United States at the International Whaling Commission conference in Brazil. After doing all these amazing things, Rebecca went to Dartmouth, but she lasted only a year and a half.

I met Rebecca during winter break when I was back in California. Having left college, she was working for a startup in Silicon Valley. Rebecca and I stayed up nearly all night talking about the challenges we faced at college. Despite being at totally different schools—one a small liberal arts school and the other in the Ivy League—we had the same frustrations. As I went back to school to start my second semester, we began exchanging emails. In one of these emails, Rebecca asked, "Why don't we just start our own college like in the movie *Accepted*?"

That conversation eventually led to me writing this book. A few days after speaking with Rebecca, I registered the domain UnCollege .org and began writing about the challenges of my college experience. I outlined my vision for a self-directed future of higher education and pitched a story to several reporters. Two bloggers picked up the story, including one at the *Chronicle of Higher Education*.

The day after the story was published, my inbox was flooded with emails.[9] At first I couldn't understand why—who reads the *Chronicle of Higher Education*? I thought. But soon I discovered that the story had been picked up by the *Huffington Post*. Before long I was fielding calls from ABC and *New York Magazine*.

By March, less than two months into my second semester, I had stopped going to classes because UnCollege was taking up all my time. I filed my withdrawal papers and shortly after officially dropped out. I moved back to San Francisco to work on UnCollege full-time. Two months after I dropped out of college, in late May, I learned that I had been selected as one of the inaugural members of the Thiel Fellowship.

The Thiel Fellowship is a program started by Peter Thiel, the cofounder of Paypal and first outside investor in Facebook, offering grants of $100,000 to young people. Anyone can apply, the only conditions are that you have to be under the age of twenty, and for two years, you can't attend a formal university. Already frustrated with the university, I decided that I would apply.

I'd first found out about the program while I was still at Hendrix. I was browsing TechCrunch when I came across an article titled "Paying Kids to Drop Out of School." My curiosity was piqued, and I found and downloaded an application. The application for the program was similar to a university application. I had to write a few essays and turn in evidence of my previous accomplishments. I was initially rejected from the program, but by then it didn't matter—UnCollege was taking off, and I'd already decided to drop out, which I did shortly thereafter. Then I got a call from the Thiel Fellowship. They were impressed with my work on UnCollege.org and wanted me to come to the final interview round. I got another call that May, after I'd been out of school nearly two months. I'd been chosen as a member of the inaugural class.

When I spoke with Peter Thiel later in the year, he told me that he was "sort of a late convert to the UnCollege idea." Peter grew up very set on a college-bound path—he took all the right AP classes in junior high and high school and then went to Stanford, where he graduated with a B.A. in philosophy. After that, he enrolled in Stanford Law School. Soon after he found himself working as an associate at Sullivan & Cromwell, a major New York law firm.

Looking back, he sees ways in which the path was screwed up, but he wasn't aware of them at the time. While in New York, Peter experienced what he calls a "quarter-life crisis" and realized that somewhere his trajectory had gone off course. Despite having done all the right things and gotten all the right credentials, Peter says he never thought about *why* he was going to college or law school. That's one of the biggest problems our educational system has—no one asks why you're going to school. From elite universities to community colleges, systems tell people that if you check these boxes off and do these things, everything will be fine. It turns out checking off boxes has nothing to do with success in life.

"I think the single biggest problem that exists with schooling," Peter told me, "is that it ends up convincing most people that they're mediocre, and then the talented people get regrouped and are forced to compete with each other, and then most of them get convinced that they're mediocre as well, and you sort of cycle and repeat, until people's dreams and aspirations are badly beaten out of them over time." The Thiel Fellowship, the program of which I'm a part, is one of Peter's attempts to fix some of these problems.

The Program for International Student Assessment (PISA) is a cross-country comparison of educational systems that aims to figure out who wins the tournament of school. The United States performs poorly on these rankings, coming in at thirtieth place, just behind Hungary and a few places above Latvia. But in spite of that, if you look around, it doesn't feel like our society is on the level of Hungary or Latvia. Perhaps the correct inference is not that schools in the United States are failing but that formal education may not matter that much at all. One of America's hidden advantages may be that we're still relatively more unschooled than many other countries in the world, even though it doesn't necessarily feel that way from inside the country.

From a financial perspective, it's interesting to think about what education is: an investment, an option, a consumer good, or an insurance product? Arguments can be made for all four, but Peter sees it as an insurance product. What is scary is that people go to school because they think it will give them an insurance policy, and then when they graduate, the insurance doesn't work. Millions of students graduate from college each year. But the reality is that there aren't millions of new jobs each year. Young college graduates expect to get decent jobs but are instead finding their degrees from Ivy League schools useless and resigning themselves to waiting tables or collecting welfare checks.

This is not a dystopian fantasy. Many college graduates are unemployed or underemployed and carry large amounts of student debt. You have the opportunity to change this. Don't use college as an insurance policy—invest in yourself. Take time to learn, travel, start projects, and do internships. You'll thank yourself when you graduate.

The people you'll meet in this book have chosen to do amazing things with their lives instead of going to college. Some people took conventional routes and still managed to get jobs at big companies like Apple or the *New York Times*. Others got creative and became filmmakers, artists, or DJs. Still others are making furniture, running a food truck, or solving the energy crisis.

These are real examples. Ariele Alasko moved across the country and now builds handmade furniture from a studio in Brooklyn.* Every piece of wood she uses is found, no exceptions, and thus totally green, combining carpentry, ecology, and art in cool ways. Across the country, a young woman named Leah started working in four-star restaurants from age fifteen to eighteen; spent three years traveling the world; and then returned to Portland, Oregon, to open a vegan, gluten-free food truck called the Heart Cart.†

Now the chief scientist of LightSail Energy, Danielle Fong dropped out of middle school in Nova Scotia after just thirty-five days. Instead, she went to Dalhousie University, graduated, and then enrolled in a PhD program at Princeton at age seventeen. She left that program after just two years and moved to Silicon Valley. After a

---

* See Ariele Alasko's blog, *Brooklyn to West*, at http://brooklyntowest.blogspot.com.

† See the Heart Cart's bog, *The Heart Cart*, at www.theheartcart.com.

couple of years of bumbling around in startups, LightSail was funded by Khosla Ventures in 2009. Along the way Danielle has spoken at the UN, presented progress reports to Bill Gates, and been recognized as a 30 Under 30 Innovator in Energy by *Forbes*. These young women are total hackers, hacking wood, hacking food, hacking energy, and making their own paths.

IS COLLEGE WORTH IT?

Going to college is like joining a gym: It's effective only if you put in the work. If you join a gym and never work out, you'll stay weak. If you pay for college but never deeply engage, you'll stay ignorant. You should go to college only if you have the self-control to actually learn, just as if you should only join a gym if you have the self-control to actually work out. People ask me all the time, who should and shouldn't go to college? There is only one definitive answer of who shouldn't go to college: those who don't want to go to college.

The converse of that statement is also true. You should go to college only if you want to go to college and know exactly why you are going to college.

In the introduction, I told you a little bit about the hacks. This is the first. It is designed to help you think about how your talents translate into real-world skills and understand whether college is the right choice for you.

Figure Out Why You're Here

Sandee Kastrul runs I.C. Stars, a nonprofit based in Chicago that helps inner-city youth who have dropped out of school get jobs at technology firms. When I asked Sandee how she helps people who can't think beyond their current environment (whether that is because they don't know where they will eat their next meal or because they have their nose buried in a book), she explained that she has her students complete the following exercise:

1. What are you on this planet to do? The answer is one word, and always a verb. Sandee's answer is to *teach*. Write down your verb.

2. What are your five greatest gifts, the things you do that support that mission? They are also verbs. Sandee's are to inspire, to listen, to lead, to love, and to sing. Each one of these verbs helps with her purpose. Write down your five greatest gifts.

3. For each gift, come up with two ways that you could use it to add value to the world. You should have a list of ten possible occupations that use your gifts. Sandee's are:

Public speaker	CEO
Community organizer	Artist
Counselor	Designer
Music critic	Singer
Project manager	Teacher

Write down your ten possible occupations:

1.   6.

2.   7.

3.   8.

4.   9.

5.   10.

4. For one of these professions, come up with five ways you can fortify that gift in the real world. For example, to become a music critic, Sandee could go to an opera, go to a music store, start practicing piano, plan a trip to Italy, and sign up for a music class. Choose one of the professions you wrote down and list five ways you can fortify this gift.

1.

2.

3.

4.

5.

5. Look back over your lists. Do you need a college degree to do—or become—the things you've come up with? If the answer is no, then you should consider how you can practice your gifts in the real world. If the answer is yes, think again. There are very few professions that actually require you go through entirely formalized training. Look for ways that learn outside the classroom. Of course, if you're paying exorbitantly for a university, that changes the equation a little bit. More on that later.

||||||||||||||||||||||||||||||||||||||||||||||||||||||||||||||||||||||||||||||||||||||||||||||||||||||||||||||||

CHAPTER TWO

The Hackademic Mind-Set

Everybody is a genius. But if you judge a fish by its ability to climb a
tree, it will spend its whole life believing that it is stupid.

—ALBERT EINSTEIN

WHEN I WAS ELEVEN YEARS OLD, I TOLD MY PARENTS I DIDN'T WANT TO
go to school. They laughed—after all, who wants to go to school in
the fifth grade?

But I wasn't kidding. I insisted that school wasn't the place for
me. Doodling and filling out worksheets bored me. Instead of teaching, my teachers spent most of their time dispensing punishments.
At the time, my mom was a public school teacher. She'd gotten into
teaching because she saw school as a social equalizer, an opportunity
for anyone to get ahead. That's exactly what school had done for her:
Working hard and getting good grades allowed her to be the first in
her disadvantaged family to go to college.

My dad wasn't exactly a fan of the idea of me leaving school either.
An engineer with an extremely logical mind, he didn't believe in

shortcuts, just the system. If there are hoops, he thinks, you just have to jump through them. But my young mind saw the problem a bit differently. Why, I thought, should I go to school if I'm not learning anything? I found an ad in our local newspaper for a "Not Back to School Night" hosted by local unschoolers. I was intrigued, and convinced my parents to take me.

There, I met people who gave us a framework and vocabulary for the educational philosophy I was just beginning to understand. These people were unschoolers, the self-directed form of homeschoolers. These young people had all been given the choice of whether they wanted to go to school. Some did, some didn't, and over the years they often floated in and out of the system at their own pace.

Unschoolers differed from homeschoolers in several distinct ways. They didn't replicate school at home. To learn geometry they didn't just sit down with worksheets—instead, they made a quilt. They didn't take standardized tests and receive arbitrary grades. Instead, they learned to write self-evaluations. At the same time, they weren't sheltered from society. They learned about evolution and sex ed like everyone else.

Meeting these unschoolers proved to my parents that I could really learn and still have a social life outside school. So they allowed me to give it a try. The worst that can happen, they reasoned, was that I wouldn't like it and would go back to school. As long as I learned something in the process, it wouldn't be a waste of time. The power to make my own decisions at an age when most parents think their kids should be seen and not heard is, to this day, the greatest gift my parents have ever given me.

ONE OF THE FIRST UNSCHOOLERS

By the time I began unschooling, the movement had been around for about thirty years. Filmmaker Astra Taylor, known for her 2005 film *Žižek!*, was among the first wave of unschoolers, part of the group in the 1970s that received John Holt's magazine *Growing Without Schooling* in the mail. Astra recalled that in those days, "The magazine was delivered to your mailbox in a brown paper bag, as though its pages contained something as controversial or shameful as pornography." Yet the conversations about the role of school in society were mainstream: A. S. Neill's *Summerhill School*, about a self-directed school in England, sold *three million copies* between 1960 and 1973.

Growing up in Athens, Georgia, Astra was in the minority as a home learner where most people went to public school. "The difference," Astra said, "is that my parents trusted me to be curious. And that's really what this entire debate is about. Have you ever met someone who isn't interested in something? Obviously sometimes people's interests aren't interesting to you—but that's a different problem. Do we need to teach babies to speak or walk?"

What's amazing is that the mainstream has been forced to admit that learning outside school is massively successful. People educated at home do better on standardized tests.[1] We are well behaved.[2] We get along well with others. Ivy League universities hunt down home-schoolers and unschoolers.[3] Stanford, Princeton, and other schools have admission counselors focused on recruiting those who didn't go to traditional schools.

Astra thought she wanted to be a scientist, and because she couldn't see doing hard science at home, she enrolled in ninth grade. After thirteen years of unschooling, public school was quite a shock. And although she could have gone home—her parents would have welcomed her—Astra stayed in school because, as she said, society told her she "would fall behind in adult life" if she didn't go to college. This was in the early 1990s when colleges hadn't yet discovered unschoolers.

She was not stimulated intellectually in school. She read more books the months before public school than during the entire three years she spent in the system. She held out for life after graduation because college was supposed to be better. Astra went to Brown University, the most liberal university in the Ivy League, a place everyone assured her she would belong.

"I realized my mistake the first day at Brown," Astra recalled, "when the administrators assembled the entire freshman class in the auditorium. 'You are all the most smart and capable of your generation,' they told us. I knew what they were saying wasn't true. I knew we weren't the smartest or the best. I had this suspicion that we were the cowards of our class—the brownnosers, the grade mongers, the play-by-the-rulers, the approval seekers. We had hustled for As, submitted to the system, and were too spineless to rock the boat. I was surrounded by a ghetto of my peers even more isolated than I was in high school. One afternoon I was complaining to a friend about my unhappiness, a friend who doesn't know his father, whose mom was in jail, who had been raised in a housing project, who didn't have the chance to go to college. He was an unschooler by necessity rather than by choice. And now he's the CTO of a major public technology company."

"He asked why I was attached to getting a degree in physics," Astra recalled. "He pointed out that I didn't engage with the material outside of class. Our conversation forced me to ask uncomfortable questions. How does someone who has embraced unschooling measure success? Why had I felt compelled to enroll in an Ivy League school? I had seen articles in *Growing Without Schooling* about unschoolers who had gone to Harvard. I thought I would do the same and that would show all the cynics. But is that what unschooling is about: finding a back door to traditional academic accolades?"

What Astra discovered that year at Brown is that unschooling is a lifelong commitment. It's not something you do until you're eighteen. It's not a stepping-stone before college. It's an ethos. She realized it was her duty to take the reins of her education. Astra left Brown after one year and returned to Georgia, but when she left, people told her she was ruining her life. "I figured out some loopholes in the system," she said, "and was able to figure out how to graduate from a state university in a year."

Astra's account resonates with my experience. I was given the space to follow my own curiosity and seek out meaningful connections with people. Most of what I learned about how to educate myself came from my unschooling peers. I joined an already existing community of about twenty unschoolers who shared their knowledge about self-education. I learned how to set goals, find learning resources, and convince people to let me work with them despite my age.

That's what I did instead of school. I didn't go to middle or high school and enjoyed six glorious years outside the classroom. I never once missed it. While other kids my age sat in class, I organized collaborative learning groups, found mentors, took college classes, lived in France, worked at startup companies, helped political campaigns, and started my own businesses.

Unschooling is an educational philosophy that values learning over schooling. It's just one part of the broader hackademic movement in which people value accomplishments over grades. Over and over again the hackademics I interviewed for this book emphasized that their grades don't matter. What matters far more is what you do in the real world. As one put it, "You need to stop giving a shit about grades and start building things."

In this chapter, I'm going to share some of the most valuable things I've learned from them and other hackademics. By the time you finish this chapter, you'll know how to set your own goals and hold yourself accountable for pursuing them. You'll also know how to build a website to show off your accomplishments and create opportunities by connecting with others. You'll even know how to throw an awesome party. Not bad for an afternoon's reading.

SLEEP HYGIENE

But let's start simple. One of the first tricks I learned about self-education was surprisingly basic—get up early.

I've always been a morning person. It doesn't matter if I've just flown eighteen hours the day before or if it's Christmas morning, I still get up at 6:00 a.m. The first day of unschooling I arose early and was starting on my "school" work by 7:00. Four hours later, I exclaimed to my mom, "I've learned more today than I did in all of the fifth grade!" And before lunch.

In short, the advantage to getting up at 6:00 is productivity. When you're the only one up, there are fewer distractions. For most of my life, I've consistently gotten up at 6:00—no earlier, no later. I set an alarm every night, but it rarely wakes me up. Usually I wake up a few minutes before the alarm, calmly climb out of bed, and turn it off. No matter when I go to bed I usually get up at 6:00. It's weird, I know.

The three to four hours I have before most people are awake are the most productive hours of my day. Those morning hours are when I did most of the work as an unschooler and when I did most of the work for UnCollege before I dropped out. When you lead a busy life—which if you don't already, you will soon—having three hours of uninterrupted work time is golden.

If you're an adolescent, there are two major forces working against you: biology and culture. Studies have shown us that adolescents naturally go to sleep and get up later, and at the same time they usually also need more sleep. Professors at Brown studied the sleep patterns of students in the ninth and tenth grades, finding that teenagers have a difficult time adapting to early school start times due to social influences and changes in their biological systems that control sleep.[4]

If that's the case, why would you exacerbate this disadvantage by staying up even later? The answer is youth (especially college) culture. When you're living in a dorm environment where everyone stays up late, you're motivated to do the same. It's not always easy to overcome these obstacles, but if you can, the rewards are tremendous. Studies have also shown that people who get up earlier are healthier and happier and tend to live longer. And, of course, are more successful.[5]

HACK OF THE DAY

Get Up at 6:00 a.m.

Every day for a week I challenge you to get up at 6:00 and spend the first few hours of your day working. It may be painful, but I promise it will also be a rewarding experience.

Here are some tips for getting up:

- As soon as you get out of bed, make yourself stand up and do ten squats. The blood will rush to your head, and you'll be awake.
- Set an alarm for a consistent time every morning. Don't hit snooze. Before you know it you'll be getting up before the alarm to turn it off.
- Drink a glass of water as soon as you get up—you're usually dehydrated after sleeping.
- Go to bed around the same time so that you get enough sleep. Try to sleep a consistent amount of time each night.
- Develop a morning routine. Many of the people I interviewed spend five minutes after getting up silently meditating.

A friend at Pepperdine University made a pledge with his fraternity brothers to get up at 6:00 a.m. At this time, one brother calls the others, creating a circle of trust and accountability. Each is motivated by the knowledge that if he doesn't get up and call his friends, their lost productivity will be his responsibility.

||||||||||||||||||||||||||||||||||||||||||||||||||||||||||||||||||||||||||||||||||||||||||||||||||||||||||||||||||||||||||||||

BE YOU

In elementary school I was one of those kids who refused to play on the playground at recess because I was paranoid about missing the bell and being late for class. Instead of enjoying myself, I'd bring a book, and sit on the asphalt on top of my room number so that I could be first in line when it came time to go back to class. Then one day in second grade, a friend said to me, "Why are you just sitting there? You're being obedient just like they want so you'll join the army."

That scared me. I didn't want to join the army. I didn't like guns, and I certainly didn't want to die. I wasn't sure if my friend was just saying that to scare me, or if she was serious, so I went to the library to do some reading.*

It turned out there was a kernel of truth in what my friend said. In the nineteenth century, American schools were modeled on the Prussian school system, which was explicitly designed to create fac-

---

* This was in 1999, before Google was ubiquitous.

tory workers and docile subjects. Government officials like Horace Mann traveled to Prussia to learn about the system and bring it back to the United States. The model was adopted in Massachusetts and quickly spread throughout the country, where it remains the basis of much of our educational system.*

This reading piqued my curiosity, and I began wondering what other lessons I was slyly being taught in school. Did I raise my hand out of respect for the teacher or did I do it because someone wanted to make me emotionally and intellectually submissive to authority figures? Did my grades show me the progress I'd made or did they just make me dependent on external validation?

I didn't really know the answers to these questions, but I resolved to retain as much of my individuality as I possibly could. To me, it seemed, school was sort of like whack-a-mole: As soon as you stood out, whether you fell behind or ran ahead, you got whacked back down to the same level.

Part of maintaining your individuality is developing self-confidence. And part of developing self-confidence is accepting that you're not going to be nice to everyone all the time. I was once with six other education entrepreneurs, crowded around a table in a dive bar in the Mission District of San Francisco, when Michael Staton, the founder of Inigral, threw out a question: "What's your special talent?"

---

* I'm not going to spend time going into this because entire books have been written on the subject. If you want a detailed history of the development of the compulsory school system in America, read John Taylor Gatto's *Dumbing Us Down* (Philadelphia: New Society, 1992).

Aron Solomon, a Canadian educator, was the first to pipe up: "I'm really good at saying, 'Fuck you.'" Everyone laughed, but Aron repeated himself. He was serious.

Gunnar Counselman, the CEO of Fidelis Education, challenged him, "Doesn't that alienate large numbers of people?"

"Yes," replied Aron, "and I don't care. The point is that you have to be so self-assured, so confident in your abilities, so sure that you will ultimately succeed that you can't care what other people think of you."

The biggest roadblock holding most of us back from the life we want is entirely self-created: It's that we care what other people think. If you feel that your actions (or lack thereof) are governed in a large part by societal expectations, the first step to not caring what other people think is to acknowledge that this is a serious problem and probably the most serious problem in your life. It's stopping you from meeting the guy or girl of your dreams. It's holding you back from making that elevator pitch. It's preventing you from following your passion and changing the world because you choose to define yourself by what other people think. You're worried that society may judge or look down on your efforts.

It's important to note here that Aron did not mean that you should ignore other people. I'm not suggesting that you disregard the opinions of anyone but yourself. I'm not suggesting that you should be a pompous ass. What I am suggesting is that you make authenticity a priority. That you have the courage to act with your own convictions. You might not expect this, but Aron is one of the best listeners I have ever met. He empathizes with the people he speaks with and understands their concerns. He takes what they say into account, but at the end of the day he makes his own decisions.

By making authenticity the top priority, you'll grant yourself the permission, time, and energy required to learn to be yourself. You can't count on anyone but yourself. Friends aren't forever, divorces are more common than ever, and families fall apart. The only person guaranteed to be by your side through all the ups and downs, from first kick to last bucket, is you.

This means that the only person you need validation from is yourself. Think about this for a moment. It only matters what *you* think. You're here on earth for a reason. You have a passion. But most of us see life as something to endure rather than enjoy, and it's because we let ourselves be controlled by the expectations of the world instead of being our own driving force.

Consider these questions a moment:

1. Would you date yourself?
2. Would you be in your own band?
3. Would you trust yourself?
4. Would you hire yourself?
5. Would you invite yourself to your party?
6. Would you recommend yourself?

If the answer to any of these questions is no, you need to start loving yourself. One of my favorite books as a child was *I Love Me*. The star of the book, an overweight female pig, would start every morning by standing in front of the mirror naked and saying, "I love me." She encountered people on her adventures that would tell her off, make fun of her, and call her fat, but she didn't care what they thought because she loved herself.

The most exciting (and arguably important) skill you can develop in life is learning to be yourself. Authenticity is a learnable skill, but learning requires action. Remember that no matter what you say, how you act, what you do, how you dress, or what your opinions are, you will polarize people. Come to expect trolls—and enjoy them. Be yourself and make friends with those who both support and challenge you. Have the courage to be you.

HACK OF THE DAY ||||||||||||||||||||

Rejection!

Because we often care too much about what other people think, we're going to practice getting rejected. Over the course of this experiment you'll learn to fail and be less afraid of the social expectations that restrict our lives. Here's what to do:

1. Get rejected every day for a week. The only requirement is that you must be rejected by a real person in the real world. Online rejections do not count. Here are some ideas for how to be rejected. Try to get rejected a new way every day.

   a. Ask someone to give you their seat in a public area without explaining why.

   b. Ask a random person on the street for $100.

c. Go outside and ask the first person you meet, "Will you go on a date with me?"

d. Go into a store and ask if it's all right to explore an area marked "Authorized Personnel Only."

e. Ask someone on the street if you can take a picture with them.

f. Take a stack of paper into the street and ask someone to help you fold paper airplanes.

2. Write for five minutes about how the experiences of being rejected made you feel. Did it get easier as the week went by?

||||||||||||||||||||||||||||||||||||||||||||||||||||||||||||||||||||||||||||||||||||||||||||||||||||||||

DO YOU LIKE MARSHMALLOWS?

I need you to find two marshmallows. Once you've obtained two marshmallows—or some equivalent sweet treat that you like—I have a question for you: Would you rather eat one marshmallow now, or wait fifteen minutes and eat both marshmallows?

Ready? Set a timer for fifteen minutes, then press start. The decision is yours. If you eat one marshmallow anytime before the fifteen minutes is up, you must throw away the second marshmallow. But if you wait the entire fifteen minutes you get to eat both marshmallows. In fifteen minutes, come back to the book and circle your result below:

I ate one marshmallow.   I waited fifteen minutes
                             and ate both.

In the 1960s, psychologists at Stanford University asked a group of four-year-olds the same question. The average child was able to resist the treat less than three minutes before giving in and eating the marshmallow. About 30 percent of the kids, however, were able to delay gratification for fifteen minutes and were rewarded with a second marshmallow.

As the children progressed in school, researchers began to notice a correlation in their ability to delay gratification for the second marshmallow and their academic performance. Self-control, it seemed, was an accurate predictor of success. Researchers surveyed parents, teachers, and friends on different traits, from how well they got along with other children to their SAT scores.

When researchers analyzed the results, they found that the children who couldn't wait the fifteen minutes had more behavior problems, struggled under stress, and had difficulty maintaining friendships. The children who waited the fifteen minutes performed better in the situations just described and scored an average 210 points higher on the SAT than their peers who could wait only thirty seconds.[6] Now, I certainly don't endorse SAT scores as a measure of academic performance, but if self-control can improve your performance on the SAT, it can improve your performance in more important areas of your life.

Max Weisel is one of the types who chose to delay gratification, but he wasn't always. Max barely graduated from high school because he couldn't see how high school would contribute to his life. He spent his high school days making music or playing video games instead of learning. Rejected from his dream school (MIT), Max shipped off to the University of Arizona. He reasoned that if he couldn't go to his dream school, then he'd choose the school that would require the least effort on his part and allow him the most time to do whatever he wanted. He lasted one semester.

What kicked Max into gear was the opportunity to work on an album with Bjork, an Icelandic musician known for flamboyant shows. Max had dabbled in development and contributed to some open-source projects, but he wasn't an expert. He'd created an iPhone app called Soundrop. Bjork contacted Max because he was the developer of this app. At first Max thought it was a joke and ignored her email for a few days. Only a few days later did he check the validity of the email.

The project would require building iPad apps with rich visual and music synthesis, which Max readily admitted to me that he "didn't really know how to do," but it sounded like an amazing opportunity, and Max said he would take on the project.

Max went from gobbling marshmallows (goofing around in college) as fast as he could to pushing the plate away and developing iPad apps. Why? Because, for the first time, he could view his work in terms of tangible results. He understood what the outcome would be if he completed the project. He wouldn't just be getting a meaningless report card; he was building something thousands of people would use. And by dropping out of school, Max had more time to work on what interested him. Going to school for five to eight hours per day took away crucial time Max needed to concentrate and maintain a healthy mental state. Dropping out gave him that time back. It was an infinite winter vacation.

Bjork hired Max to build custom iPad apps for each of the songs on her new album. In the spring of 2012, Max was invited to go on tour with Bjork and had the opportunity to visit five continents. While he was on tour, MIT called, offering Max a residency at their famed Media Lab. He thought to himself, if the Media Lab wants me, I must be doing something right.

Now, instead of paying for college, Max is making more money than his parents—combined. But, Max tells me, it hasn't been easy. He's worked harder since dropping out of college than he ever has before. Learning to develop iPad apps that do things with sound and animation that no one had ever done before is one of the biggest challenges that Max has ever accepted. To be sure, Max is having fun, but he's certainly not playing video games all day. He chose to delay gratification and not goof around in college because he knew that there would be greater rewards in the future.

Taking control of your education means that you have no one to blame but yourself. No one at all. You can't blame your professors. Or your parents. Or your peers. You are responsible for your own successes and failures. Taking on projects that you don't know how to do is a fabulous way to ensure that you're always learning. In this way, you challenge yourself and ensure that you don't just eat the marshmallow.

Building Self-Control

Everyone eats sugar. Today's exercise for building self-control is to limit your sugar intake.

1. On Saturday, ban yourself from eating sugar. None of it. No dessert. No sugar in your coffee.
2. Do this for two weeks. The following week, don't eat sugar on Wednesday or Saturday. None.
3. Do this for two weeks, and then add in Monday. No sugar on Saturday, Monday, or Wednesday. If a friend offers you dessert, tell them you're practicing self-control.
4. Do this for one week, and then go for another week without eating any sugar. No sugar for an entire week.

LEARNING OUTSIDE THE CLASSROOM

Everyone says you should make to-do lists to help you organize your actionable tasks. To-do lists are great. I use a task manager called Things. But to-do lists are very limiting; they let you see only a very narrow picture of what you have to do.

When I pick up a legal pad and my favorite pen, you know I'm making a real list. This is not a list of things I need to do today, this week, or next. This is a list of things I want to learn.

The beauty of a to-learn list is that it's never finished. You can never check everything off because there's always more to learn.

Writing a to-learn list is the first step in understanding that education is lifewide and progress is lifelong.

If you're having trouble thinking of what you'd put on your to-learn list, don't worry. One downside of school is that we're never asked what we're interested in. Think about it: In your twelve years of school, did any teachers ever ask you what you wanted to learn or did they just prepare you for the next test?

The reality is that learning isn't just about preparing for the next test. We're naturally curious. As babies we seek to explore the world. Then as we grow, and enter school, much of that intellectual curiosity is beaten out of us, largely because we're never asked what we want to learn.

Countless studies have shown that children, when given more autonomy to learn on their own, show themselves to be more competent and express a greater sense of self-worth. Extrinsic rewards—such as grades, that traditional schooling relies on wholeheartedly—depress students' desire to learn on their own. When students are given control of their own education, they are motivated to learn for their own sake.[7]

One argument I hear often is that if you pull a child out of school, he or she will just play video games, or mess around with Legos, or find some other way to be generally unproductive. In the unschooling world this happens all the time. It happens often enough that the process is considered normal, and there's even a name for it: *deschooling.*

Deschooling is the process by which an individual who has been in school reacclimatizes to the natural world and figures out what he or she wants to learn. Usually this process takes a few weeks, and it is necessary for someone to engage in whatever activity he deems to be fun and interesting before he realizes he has the freedom to choose his interests.

Once you realize you're playing video games because you want to, not because anybody else told you to, you begin to realize that you can do other things *because you want to.* Soon the curiosity comes back to the child who has just left school and he begins asking questions, exploring, and learning from the world.

The point of making a to-learn list is so that once you figure out that you can do things because you want to, not because your teacher said you should, you can go out and start learning.

At the NBC News Education Nation event in New York City in September 2011 there was a panel composed of students, and the moderator asked, "What's your favorite class?" The first student immediately answered, "History class is my favorite because my teacher makes it fun!"

The moderator replied, with complete sincerity, "But if you're having fun, how are you learning?" This is a perfect example of the type of viewpoint we're fighting against.

Writing a to-learn list enables you to engage in what is known in pedagogical sciences as project-based learning. Project-based learning is a style of teaching in which students define problems they are interested in and then solve them with guidance from their teacher. Across the board, learning outcomes from student-centric learning approaches and problem-based learning are higher than from traditional lecture models.

In 1992, a study used open-ended questionnaires to prove that when students are interested in the material they are learning, they are more likely to both remember the information and expand on the information learned. By using open-ended questionnaires to discover the interests of students in the fifth and sixth grades, problems were created that were tailored specifically to those interests. Students were then tested on reading comprehension and math with questions both to their interest and not. For the reading questions that related to a student's interest, students were:

> more likely to recall more points, recall information from more paragraphs, recall more topic sentences, write more sentences, provide more detailed information about topics read, have no errors on their written recall, and provide additional topic-relevant information.[8]

However, in this study, students showed little difference when doing math problems due to the lack of depth in the problem. In another study, however, when using more specifically designed math problems, students showed a significant increase in math performance when problems were catered to the students' interests.[9]

No shit. Did we really need scientists to tell us this? It's pretty obvious that people perform better when they are interested in what they are doing. Duh.

The To-Learn List

If you aren't getting to learn what you want in the classroom—which you probably aren't because very few schools have adopted the approach of asking students what they're interested in—writing a to-learn list will enable you to engage in project-based learning on your own terms.

1. Write a to-learn list. Take ten minutes and write down everything you want to learn more about.

   Here's my list of what I want to learn:

German	Python
Design	How to cook Indian food
Flying	Finance
Neuroscience	Life in a developing country
Linguistics	

2. That's a good start, but some of the things you wrote down are quite broad. I wrote down "design" but that is a huge subject. What is it that I really want to learn? How to design a font? How to use Photoshop to create web pages? How to implement design thinking? Go through your to-learn list and make your broad interests more precise. Do I just want to learn Python? No, I want to learn Python to build a web application. When you finish you'll have an awesome idea of where to start to learn new material. Learning effectively starts by learning what you're interested in. Here's my refined list:

Learn to order food in German

Learn to design a typeface

Learn to fly a single-engine airplane

Learn enough neuroscience so I can read scientific papers on the subject

Learn how to tell the etymology of words

Learn to build a web application in Python

Learn how to make naan

Learn how to evaluate stock risk

Learn how to live on $10 per day

3. Choose one of the things you want to learn, and get started. Take an hour to order a book on the subject or email a friend who can help point you where to start learning.

||||||||||||||||||||||||||||||||||||||||||||||||||||||||||||||||||||||||||||||||||||||||||||||||||||||||||||||||

PEER ACCOUNTABILITY

One of the biggest challenges of self-education is finding ways to keep yourself motivated. When you don't have a teacher checking in to make sure you're doing your homework, you have to find other ways to keep yourself accountable. Telling the world about your goals is one way; peer accountability is another. By sharing your goals with a group of your peers you create a system of peer accountability.

Every week you can meet with your peers and check in on the progress everyone has made.

When writing this book I began searching the world for what I considered good academic environments—places where students are independent critical thinkers; work on group projects, not individual tests; and make their own decisions about what to learn. The Center for Research and Interdisciplinarity (CRI), a part of the Sorbonne in Paris that awards accredited bachelor's, master's, and doctoral degrees, operates in this fashion. Students meet every Friday to set goals and spend the rest of the time directing their own education. If I wanted to study biology, this is where I would do it.

The center is the brainchild of François Taddei, a man of forty who, if he stuck his tongue out, could pass for Albert Einstein. François is an evolutionary biologist by training. He's not supposed to know anything about education or pedagogy. What's fascinating, he told me, is that his interest is not personal; he had a fabulous time in school. François did everything right by French academic standards. He aced the BAC (the equivalent of our SAT), finished high school early, and by age eighteen knew that he had guaranteed himself a tenured position in the French academic system.

That knowledge would make many people complacent. Not so with François. Despite his great success, he has lost no enthusiasm about finding ways to hack the system he came up through. The French school system is highly tracked. From the age of thirteen or fourteen, students take tests that determine whether they will go to university. Once a student chooses a major, it is very difficult to change, and even experts in related fields (such as chemistry and biology) rarely interact with each other.

François started the CRI to address the lack of collaboration between fields. He literally occupied the third floor of a building and hacked it into a research lab. During the renovation of a 1960s-era building at the Sorbonne, François and his students moved in and took over, like squatters. And the university has been unable to evict François because he is a tenured professor. The building itself has all the charm of a disused warehouse. The plumbing in the bathrooms is completely exposed and rusted. But when you enter the CRI the atmosphere changes. There is a constant hubbub of voices. Posters hang on the wall, detailing the success of the students. And success they have had.

For the last three years straight, students from the CRI have won the iGEM competition in synthetic biology. They've beaten out the teams from Oxford, MIT, and Caltech. How, you ask? Well, they have an environment that fosters collaboration instead of competition. And some of their students left these other institutions specifically to work in this magical lab in Paris.

Because the CRI is so nontraditional, funding for the center doesn't come from the Sorbonne. Instead, François has secured funding from the Bettencourt Foundation, the largest foundation in France. In fact, the CRI has its own nonprofit organization so it can skirt around the budgeting of the university.

What's unique is that there is only one required class per week— and the students lead it. Every week, students get together to talk about what they've learned since the last meeting and set goals for the upcoming week. Outside of that one required goal-setting session, students direct their own projects. They take time away from the center to do internships and work in other labs. What's even more amazing is that the students who engage in self-directed learning at the CRI earn degrees from the Sorbonne—one of the most prestigious universities in France.

François refuses to give grades. Although he grudgingly turns grades in when the university demands it, he does not reveal the grades to the students.

Children's intrinsic motivation declines every year over the course of traditional schooling. There are many reasons for this, but the main reason, science has continually shown, is that traditional education relies too heavily on grades to motivate students. From preschool children[10] to college students,[11] extrinsic rewards shunt motivation to learn on one's own.

As an unschooler, I had learning groups that functioned in similar ways to the learning groups at the CRI. On a weekly basis, my peers and I would get together to set and share our goals. The following week we'd follow up and evaluate our progress. But when I left college I no longer had weekly meetings with my fellow unschoolers, so I had to develop alternative systems of accountability.

One system to keep myself accountable arose a few months after I left college, when I had coffee with my friend Eden Full. Eden, like me, is a Thiel Fellow and college dropout. Unlike me, however, Eden left a prestigious institution—Princeton—to develop a solar solution for developing countries. Her contraption, which she calls the sun saluter, is a low-cost way to rotate solar panels to face the sun, thereby increasing their efficiency. It's pretty smart.

When we met for coffee we were both going a little crazy from traveling. I had just gotten back from Chicago, and Eden from Amsterdam. I had spoken at a conference, and Eden won a business plan competition in the Netherlands that awarded her €200,000—not bad for a weekend's work. But those weren't our only trips. I was flying to New York the following week, and Eden to Indonesia, followed by Los Angeles and Paris, respectively. As we compared travel schedules, trying to figure out if we would ever be in the same place, Eden blurted, "Dale, how do you stay productive?"

Before Eden asked me, I'd never really taken time to think about this question, but when I did, I realized I had built dozens of systems over my years as an unschooler that keep me organized, productive, and on task.

"What do you use to track your to-do list?" I asked.

"I don't," Eden replied.

Keeping track of—and more important writing down—your to-do list is one of the fundamental productivity tools I use. I first got into the habit of writing to-do lists as an unschooler. Every morning I would write down my goals for the day on a sticky note. Sticky notes have limited usage, so today I use an application called Things—it beautifully syncs across my MacBook Air, iPad, and iPhone. I use to-do lists because it frees up the brain space that I would use to keep track of to-do items for other things, which means I am generally more productive.

Tracking to-dos does not have to be done on a computer; using paper and pen works just as well. It's a matter of personal preference and developing a system that works for you. There are entire books written on this subject, such as Scott Belsky's *Making Ideas Happen*[12] and David Allen's *Getting Things Done.*[13] The main takeaway is this: Make to-do items actionable by starting each item with a verb. For example, instead of writing "presentation for client X" write "create presentation for client X."

If you're interested in reading more, pick up one of the books I mentioned because I'm not going to dwell on details here. The bottom line is this: Some sort of tracking method is better than none. Everyone figures out the nuances of her own system, choosing her own system (whether on paper or screen), and decides on her own syntax (verb or not). Some people I know use Gmail's smart filters combined with labels to create a to-do mailbox. Whatever works best for you, run with it—write down your to-do list to free up brain space.

One problem with keeping to-do lists is that there's no accountability. If you don't complete a task, there's no one to hold you responsible but yourself. It's often far too easy to put off a task until tomorrow instead of completing it today.

"Have you ever had an accountability buddy?" I asked Eden.

Every week, I share my goals for the week with some of my friends and they share their goals with me. Although we work independently, it means that we have someone to be accountable to. One daily goal I have is to write a thousand words. If I don't write my thousand words for the day, someone is there to check in on me.

Eden and I became accountability buddies. Since August we've been exchanging our goals every week. When I am putting off writing, Eden bugs me about it. When she hasn't written a product spec for the week, she hears from me. Together, we push each other.

Accountability Buddy

With an accountability buddy you exchange five to ten high-level goals for the week. The following week you check in with each other to make sure that you've met your goals for the week.

1. Email two to three of your friends to ask if they will exchange weekly goals with you. Make it clear that this won't take a lot of time, and you will be helping each other in the process.
2. Once a week on a set day (I suggest Sunday), email your friends your goals.
3. If possible, on the same day, meet your friends for coffee or have a quick phone call to talk about what you achieved the previous week. You'll ask each other if you completed your goals for the previous week and help each other set future goals. If you haven't finished a goal, it goes back on your list.

For example, this is the list I sent Eden one week in October:

Conduct five interviews

Write one thousand words per day

Write speech for EBS conference

Write CNN op-ed
Write NYT learning blog guest post

4. If you really can't find anyone, I'll be your accountability buddy. Email your goals for the week to todo@uncollege.org with "Accountability Buddy" in the subject line, and I'll respond with mine. I keep my life open and transparent.

|||||||||||||||||||||||||||||||||||||||||||||||||||||||||||||||||||||||||||||||||||||||||||||||||||||||||||||||

PUTTING YOURSELF OUT THERE

Finding an accountability buddy to tell about your progress is a great first step, but you also have to find a way to communicate to the world what you're learning. The best way to do this is to create a personal website that functions as a portfolio of your work. Alex MacCaw is a prime example of someone who skipped college and used a personal website to land a job.

As he scanned his badge and opened the door to the Twitter corporate cafeteria, Alex said to me in a lilting London accent, "I'm the first MacCaw not to go to Cambridge." Given that Alex went to boarding school, the epitome of traditional education, at age eight, not going to the university is quite a statement.

His frustrations with school started at age fifteen, when his boarding school house master asked him to make a website for the school. Alex completed the site, discovered he loved programming, and began picking up freelance gigs on the Internet. He did a lot of reading and started contributing to open-source projects. One of the projects he contributed to, Juggernaut, became popular and people began approaching him asking him to consult on projects. By the time he turned sixteen he figured out that he was making more than his teachers. Soon after taking his GCSEs Alex skipped off to London to work as a web developer for a year. He never looked back, and he never even opened the results of his GCSEs. To this day, he doesn't know how he did—he could have failed his exams completely.

At age nineteen, Alex hopped the Atlantic Ocean and settled in San Francisco working on a startup for a summer. He knew he wanted to live in California, but when it became clear that he wouldn't be able to get an H-1B visa, a normal immigrant visa, without a degree he began exploring other options. He discovered that he could qualify for an O-1 visa without a degree, but to obtain that visa he would have to do something notable.

Alex's goal—move to San Francisco—turned out to be more complicated than he imagined. But Alex knew that he could achieve that goal if he broke it down into small enough steps. His thought process was this:

1. I want to move to San Francisco.
2. To do that I need an O-1 visa.
3. To get an O-1 visa I need to qualify as an "extraordinary individual."
4. To be an extraordinary individual I need to write a book or get lots of press.

After some initial setbacks, Alex approached O'Reilly Media, a technology book publisher, about writing a book. He met someone at a Google party in San Francisco who offered to introduce him to an editor at O'Rielly. That person asked him to write a proposal, which Alex did. He eventually convinced them to give him a book contract for the book *JavaScript Web Applications* because of his contributions to open-source projects.

It took a year and seventeen countries to do it. Alex's journey took him from South Africa to Japan to Peru to New Zealand. What Alex loved about traveling is that it "gave him time to think." But he didn't spend too much time just traveling; he also finished his book, got it published, and began searching for companies that would be willing to sponsor an O-1 visa.

Today, Alex works at Twitter. How Alex got hired at a tech company without a degree is pretty standard—it's the way everyone gets hired at technology companies. He created a portfolio on his website (alexmaccaw.co.uk) and provided links to his StackOverflow and GitHub accounts where he hosted examples of projects that he had built so that his prospective employers could see examples of his coding skills.

Creating a personal website and online portfolio is the same way I got hired at Zinch when I was eighteen. I first registered the domain dalejstephens.com when I was about sixteen and began writing about my experiences. It turned into an online portfolio of my work where I could show off my accomplishments—everything from the library I helped build to the time I spent in France to the photography business I owned.

The reason I was able to help build a library, work on political campaigns, and get internships at startups was because I knew how to communicate my talents. My website was not just a blog but rather a portfolio that communicated what value I bring to the world. It showed off my super powers. My home page contained a three-hundred-word biography I wrote about myself in which I mentioned the different projects I was involved with—like the library, politics, and startups. I linked to individual pages on which I detailed what I had done for each of those projects, what I had learned, and what I had become an expert in by working on that project. I also had another page called "Skills" on which on listed my exact skills and linked to pages detailing how I had learned each skill.

Because self-education doesn't come with a degree, it's important that you take the time to reflect and share your knowledge so that the world knows you're learning. If you don't share what you've learned, people might assume you spend your days goofing off and playing video games. You can write blog posts about what you're learning, make lists of the books you're reading, and create portfolios that show off your accomplishments.

HACK OF THE DAY ||||||||||||||||||||||

Get a Personal Website

Everyone should have a personal website to use as a portfolio whether or not you have a college degree. It may seem daunting to create a website if you're unfamiliar with the web, but I'm going to break it down into a few simple steps:

1. Register a domain that includes your name like dalejstephens .com. You can do this somewhere such as NameCheap. This

should cost you about $8 annually. If yourname.com isn't available, try .net, .me, or add your middle initial.

2. Now you have two options:

    a. You can take the easy route and create a website with About.me, WordPress, or Tumblr.

    b. Or you can build a website from scratch.

3. I'm going to concentrate on the first option. Any of the above-listed sites allow you to create a personal website with no coding experience. I'm going to focus on About.me because it is the easiest to start with, but I suggest you move to WordPress or Tumblr when you have more time. About.me is a free service that allows you to create personal websites. It is not as customizable as WordPress or Tumblr but the setup process is simpler. Create an account on About.me and follow the directions to set up your custom domain name. From there you can add a professional bio and links to LinkedIn, Facebook, and Twitter.

4. When you get more time, set up a WordPress or Tumblr account and redirect your custom domain name to that page. Create pages such as "Projects," "Reading List," "Goals," and "Friends" to provide more content. Use one of the pages as a blog and write about what you're learning.

5. The most important page to create is a page called "Skills" in which you outline your specific skills. Think of this page as a résumé, but instead of organizing it chronologically, organize it by what you can do. What your talents are. Choose skills that encompass your knowledge.

Mine are:

- Starting things—this involves businesses and projects I've started
- Project management—this involves companies I've worked for
- Storytelling—this includes writing, speaking, and marketing

If you don't know what your skills are, start with the obvious one: learning! We're *all* skilled at learning, and a lot of what you've done up until this point falls into that bucket. You can also be more specific. Are you skilled at research? Statistics? Analysis? Write it down, and make sure you explain *how* you learned that skill. It's not good enough to just say you're talented—you have to be ready to back up your statements.

||||||||||||||||||||||||||||||||||||||||||||||||||||||||||||||||||||||||||||||||||||||||||||||||||||||||

ORGANIZING COLLABORATIVE LEARNING GROUPS

The highlight of unschooling was organizing collaborative learning groups with my friends. Once per week we'd get together to discuss a chosen topic. Usually, this was consistent week after week. For example, my French group would meet on Fridays while my English group would meet on Tuesdays. The structure of these groups varied. In the French group we simply got together and spoke about our weeks and news of the day in French. In the English group we actually got together at the beginning of the year and set out a syllabus and decided what books we would read over the course of the year.

These groups are a lot like book clubs, but they aren't limited to discussing literature. You can speak French, make sushi, or practice making pottery. The subject material that you practice is irrelevant—the point is that you're doing it with other people in the real world.

This camaraderie is what I think is lost with online education. Don't get me wrong—online education is wonderful. OpenCourse-Ware and the Khan Academy have made great progress in democratizing knowledge, but there is a distinct difference between knowledge and education. Anyone can learn facts from anywhere. Anyone can go to the library. Anyone can use Google. The knowledge is there. It's free. And it's not hard to find.

The biggest value of going to a university is that they have a monopoly on young talent. At top-tier universities you'll find smart and interesting people who will support, challenge, and share your ideas. They'll push your thinking and help you refine your conclusions.

While this process most often happens at universities, it can happen in the real world, too—you just have to organize what I call a *brain party.*

Invite a small but diverse group of friends to join you for breakfasts, lunch, or dinner at your home or somewhere it's OK to be lively. Try to include people who don't already do what you do. You can make it a potluck or provide food. I usually just buy two pizzas, and that small investment makes for a lot of happy people. The key is providing food and letting people know that you won't just be hanging out. Make sure people understand that there is an intellectual purpose to your meeting.

Start by describing what you're currently learning or working on and the challenges you're facing. Listen to what people say and write down their feedback. It won't be long before ideas are bouncing around the room.

Enforce a no-naysaying rule during the party—all ideas, even the most improbable, are valid and worthwhile. You never know where they will lead. After an hour at most, let the topic of your current project go. The group can disperse or continue as an unstructured party.

HACK OF THE DAY |||||||||||||||||||||||

Plan a Brain Party

Here are some things to consider:

- Which five friends will I invite?
- When will my brain party take place?
- What is the topic of my brain party?
- What food will I serve at my brain party?
- What challenges will we discuss at the brain party?

After the brain party, reflect on the experience. What could you have done better? Did you effectively share your challenges? How could get more value from the experience?

CHAPTER THREE

Identifying Your Talents

Live as if you were to die tomorrow.
Learn as if you were to live forever.

—MAHATMA GANDHI

IN THE MID-1990S, NEARLY FOUR HUNDRED FIFTH GRADERS IN NEW YORK public schools were given a reasonably basic nonverbal test, a bit like an easy form of an IQ test. After the students finished, researchers returned the scored tests and provided the children with a single line of feedback. The kids were randomly divided into two groups. Half of the kids were told, "You must be smart at this" and the other half were told, "You must have worked really hard." Next, the students were given the choice between two subsequent tests—one test, they were told, was more difficult; the other was an easy test. Carol Dweck, the psychologist who designed the experiment, thought the different forms of praise would have only a marginal effect. She didn't anticipate that a single line of praise could so dramatically affect the kids' choices. Nearly 90 percent of the kids praised for their effort chose the harder test, while most of the kids praised for their intelligence chose the easier test. Dweck concluded that praising kids for their intelligence encourages them to make choices that make them look smart and successful, thereby discouraging them from making mistakes and taking risks.[1]

But Dweck wasn't done; she had another round of experiments lined up for the fifth graders. This time, she gave the kids an extremely difficult test that was originally written for eighth graders. The students praised for their effort worked diligently on the test. The students praised for intelligence gave up easily. They knew they were making mistakes, and they didn't want to face the reality of failure. After finishing this task, the students were given the choice of looking at the exams of other students who performed worse or better than they did. The students praised for intelligence almost always chose to look at the test of someone who did worse, as if to bolster their self-confidence. The hardworking kids, on the other hand, chose more often to look at the exams with high scores, the ones with the correct answers. They wanted to learn from their mistakes and understand how to do better next time.

For the fourth and final test, Dweck's team of researchers gave the fifth graders a test that was the same difficulty as the original test. In theory, scores on this test should have been about the same as the first time around, but that wasn't the case. Instead, the students who were praised for being hardworking saw their scores increase by 30 percent. This result is mind-boggling by itself but even more staggering when compared to the students who were told they were smart; they saw their scores drop by nearly 20 percent.

This experiment shows that your mind-set matters when you

learn. If you're told you're smart, you begin to believe that your intelligence is static. You may think you're stuck where you are, and there is no hope for improvement. On the other hand, if you're told you're hardworking, that means that you have a growth mind-set. You believe that with enough dedication and tenacity, you can improve.

You may think this is a subtle difference, but the research shows it has a huge impact on how much and how well you'll learn. Ask your teachers, your parents, and your friends not to praise you for your intelligence but rather to praise your effort. At least once per week, ask someone to compliment you as a hard worker to remind yourself that with a little patience and effort you can learn anything.

As you might expect, the brain has a huge impact on how we learn. Not only does our mind-set impact how effectively we learn but it often predisposes us to learn in certain ways. Learning how your brain prefers to process information can make learning fun and enjoyable instead of monotonous.

In college, I had a professor who really enjoyed lecturing. Unfortunately for me, and the rest of the class, his lectures were neither stimulating nor engaging. He refused to interact with the class, and often when I put my hand up to ask a question, he'd tell me to put my hand down so that he could finish. But he never got around to answering my question or engaging with the class in any other way.

For me this type of learning—listening to a teacher lecture to fifty students—was not ideal. Most likely this professor was lectured to when he was in college, so naturally he assumed that lecturing was the appropriate way to teach. That's a silly assumption. When I was growing up, my mom had a sign hanging in her bedroom that said

"Your Children Are Not You." My college professor needed a similar reminder; I wish I'd made him a plaque that said "Your Students Are Not You."

There are many different ways to learn—some of the most common are through visual representation, lecture, text, and physical movement. We call these learning preferences visual, aural, read/write, and kinesthetic.

Back in the 1970s, scientists thought different people were naturally inclined to learn more through a particular style; for example, someone who learned 100 percent of material from reading a book would only learn 70 percent from listening to a lecture. But we now know that's not true. The average person, free from learning disabilities, learns with the same efficacy from either method. However, what is true is that learning through a method that you prefer *makes learning more enjoyable.* If you enjoy learning, *you're inclined to learn more* instead of doing the bare minimum required.

For this reason, it's important to understand how you prefer to learn. Some people really like listening to lectures. Others prefer learning visually and need to draw a concept and diagrams to understand them. Some need to write ideas down in their own words to understand them. Still others prefer learning kinesthetically and must do things with their hands before they understand concepts.

Countless people have told me stories of how they were discriminated against in school simply because of their learning preference.

One time at college, I was studying for a test with a friend who prefers learning visually and has a photographic memory. She was drawing political cartoons to remember the concepts from our international relations course. Another classmate came by with five pages of notes neatly typed and cross-referenced in Excel. Both of these individuals had discovered by accident how they prefer to learn and developed strategies to learn more efficiently and effectively. The problem is that most people discover how they learn only after many years of trial and error. What if you were immediately able to identify how you learn and use it to increase your productivity in school, work, and life?

Here's how: As I noted before, there are four basic learning preferences—visual, aural, read/write, and kinesthetic—that appear in pedagogical literature. This does not mean that different people learn better in certain ways—science shows us if you're a read/write learner, you will not comprehend more from a book than from a lecture. *However*, people do have learning preferences, and if you enjoy reading a book more than going to a lecture, you're more likely to be engaged while reading the book and bored while in the lecture.

A study done in 2001 found that when adults feel positive, their capacity for intellectual, social, and psychological resources is expanded.[2] At the end of the day, you'll learn more if you enjoy the method by which you are learning. At the same time, these options are not black and white; most people blend the four learning preferences but learn primarily through one of the media.

I've devised ten short questions to help determine your learning preference. These are simple questions and aren't meant to trick you. Choose the answer that first comes to mind; don't spend too much time thinking about any one question:

WHEN I LISTEN TO MUSIC, I . . .

A. Daydream

B. Hum or sing along

C. Look up the lyrics online

D. Tap my foot or move to the music

WHEN I'M STUDYING FOR A TEST, I . . .

A. Draw diagrams and illustrations

B. Have someone ask me questions

C. Write down questions and answers

D. Create 3-D models

WHEN I READ FOR FUN, I PREFER . . .

A. A travel book with pictures

B. An audiobook

C. A paperback

D. A DIY guide to building computers

WHEN I GO TO A SCIENCE MUSEUM, I . . .

A. Find a map of all the exhibits

B. Like to use audio guides

C. Read the signs in front of the exhibits

D. Start building things at the interactive exhibit

I WOULD RATHER GO TO A(N) . . .

A. Art class

B. History lecture

C. English class

D. Aerobics class

WHEN I'M HAPPY, I . . .

A. Smile

B. Shout and tell the world

C. Write my thoughts down in my journal

D. Jump for joy

IF I'M STANDING IN LINE AT THE MOVIES, I . . .

A. Look at the movie posters

B. Talk to the person next to me

C. Read reviews on my iPhone

D. Tap my foot or snap my fingers

WHEN SOLVING A PROBLEM, I . . .

A. Draw a brainstorming map

B. Talk to friends or experts

C. Write down my ideas

D. Visualize the problem in my mind and make note cards
for each step

TO LEARN HOW AN IPHONE WORKS, I WOULD RATHER . . .

A. Watch a movie about it

B. Listen to someone explain it

C. Read a book about it

D. Buy an old iPhone and take it apart

AFTER A PARTY, I USUALLY REMEMBER . . .

A. The faces of people there but not names

B. The names of people there but not faces

C. The first line from the book I read off the bookshelf

D. What I did while I was there

If you circled mostly As, you're a visual learner. If you circled mostly Bs, you're an aural learner. If you circled mostly Cs, you're a read/write learner. If you circled mostly Ds, you're a kinesthetic learner.

Keep in mind that these are only learning preferences. Studying in a certain fashion will not necessarily make you learn more but rather make it more enjoyable for you to learn. Figuring out how you learn best is the first step to identifying your talents. You might already be familiar with the subject you love but hate the way you're learning it. Maybe you find biology interesting, but you can't stand listening to lectures. Now that you understand how you prefer to learn, try learning biology—or any subject that you don't enjoy—in the way you learn best. Instead of listening to the lecture, pick up a book, draw models of cells, or spend more time in the laboratory. If you're wondering why you don't seem to be good at anything, you might discover that the problem is not that you aren't talented but rather that you aren't engaging your talents in meaningful ways.

OVERCOMING (YOUR OWN) EXPECTATIONS

One of the scariest parts about self-education is that you might actually discover your talents. Think about that for a moment. Have you ever considered that you might be afraid of discovering your talents? It's quite plausible you might be good at something you don't initially feel proud of. You might be good at something that disappoints your parents. You might be good at something that causes your friends to judge you. Or your talent might be in an industry where you don't fit expectations.

When I first met Tiffany Mikell, I knew she was awesome because of her frizzy hair. Tiffany grew up on the South Side of Chicago. She had everything against her—all the minority labels. As a young black single mother without a college degree, the future seemed daunting. Then she found an ad in the local paper advertising a program called I.C. Stars, a nonprofit that helps people from inner-city Chicago get jobs in the technology sector. The advertisement said they were in need of twelve "smart-ass people."

"I felt like I qualified," Tiffany told me.

Tiffany got the application and found it riddled with questions like, "Are you smart as hell?" and "Do you want to change the world?" She answered yes to all the questions except the last—"Do you love technology?" Tiffany wasn't sure if she loved technology—she'd always been more of a book person than a computer person—but she applied anyhow. She needed a break; she was twenty-one and had an infant son to support.

In fact, Tiffany had been supporting herself since she was seventeen. When she was fifteen, she became disillusioned with school and began preparing to take the GED the day she turned seventeen. She did, and she passed. She wanted to study English but bounced around between colleges because the "classes were too theoretical."

When Tiffany participated in I.C. Stars, the program was in its infancy; it was a four-month program that provided weekly life coaching. As she completed the I.C. Stars program, she would read job descriptions in the newspaper and think, *I could do this*, but then discover they required a degree and seven to ten years of work experience. "What I learned at I.C. Stars," Tiffany told me, "was how to market my skills, how to look at my life, and realize my life experience qualified me for most positions."

Toward the end of I.C. Stars, Tiffany found out about a month-long program hosted by Accenture to hire and train new employees to use Java. The program was set up to train thirty people in Java for a month and then hire seven out of that group. Tiffany applied, and Accenture promptly rejected her because she didn't have a college degree. But Tiffany didn't take no for an answer. She sent Accenture a letter back outlining her relevant experience, and they invited her back for an interview. Tiffany's experience shone through, and she got into the program.

Tiffany was the only woman in the program, the only person without a college degree, and the only black person in sight. But she didn't let that stop her from leading the class. The first day they asked for four volunteers to be project managers, and Tiffany raised her hand. "That decision," she tells me, "is what got me here today."

Although she was scared because she'd never programmed computers before, she was one of the seven hired by Accenture at the end of the program. She worked for Accenture for four and a half years. Every time she was up for a promotion, she got one, even though she had no college degree.

I asked Tiffany whether she felt as if her skin tone and gender had been the cause of adversity.

"Over and over again," Tiffany told me, "in technology work I'm either the only woman, only black person, or both. I show up to client meetings and they think I'm there to make coffee, not build a back-end database."

She laughed, saying, "I find it comical. But I see it as my personal mission to change expectations. If people see enough rock star black women writing JavaScript, perceptions will change. I'm unapologetic for who I am because I know my performance speaks for itself."

Discovering her talent for JavaScript programming was difficult for Tiffany because it was so far outside of what she expected to be good at. As a child, she was a bookworm, and at the few colleges she tried studying, she always took English classes. She thought she might be a journalist someday. Instead, Tiffany found a technical talent, and instead of dismissing it because it was in an unfamiliar field, she embraced it. Often your talents are hidden by your own limited worldview. Just because you think you don't immediately fit in—just as Tiffany didn't fit the expectation of a typical computer programmer—doesn't mean you aren't talented.

What You Aren't Talented At

If I asked you, "What are you good at?" you'd probably struggle to find an answer. That's normal, we don't catalog positive experiences. Sadly, our brains are designed to pick up on, and remember, the negative aspects of life. Our failures represent things we aren't good at—so we remember our weaknesses instead of our strengths.

1. Make a list of things you are horrible at doing—any skills that by normal standards you would be considered a miserable and horrible failure. Would you rather go Dumpster diving than finish your chemistry problem set? Write it down.

2. After you've written down fifteen areas of life in which you are a slimy failure, stop and ask yourself why. Did you fail at this because you decided before you even started that you would be a failure? Did you decide to fail because you didn't think you were qualified?

3. Identify three areas where you consider yourself untalented and commit to giving them another try. Think you're too skinny to swim? Try it again. This time, don't decide to fail before you even try.

||||||||||||||||||||||||||||||||||||||||||||||||||||||||||||||||||||||||||||||||||||||||||||||||||||

WHAT YOU DON'T KNOW

If directly facing your failures and fears by giving them another shot is too scary, you might consider trying activities or interests in which you have no experience. This way, there is no precedent, and you won't disappoint yourself if you don't succeed.

This is how Stephen Johnson navigated his way to becoming an award-winning architect after dropping out of Columbia University. Stephen was a model high school student; he got straight As and a perfect math SAT score. He did everything right and everyone assumed he was on his way to a brilliant career in mathematics. But when he got to Columbia University, he realized that wasn't what he wanted. Shortly thereafter, Stephen dropped out, moved to Greece, and tried to write a book.

After a year, Stephen returned to the United States. He didn't have any concrete plans, so he started working for a temp agency and found himself with a two-week gig at an architecture firm in Cambridge painting floors. At the end of the two weeks, as he was wheeling his bike out of the back door, his boss said, "Where are you going? Come back on Monday; we'll find something for you to do."

When he came back on Monday, the firm asked if he knew anything about architecture. Stephen admitted that he had no experience with architecture, but said he'd be willing to give it a shot. He became a full-time employee with the firm, and over seven years advanced from apprentice to designer, eventually becoming a fully licensed architect.

Today, Stephen is an award-winning architect who has led the development of landmark civic projects for over three decades. His projects have won five national American Institute of Architects (AIA) awards. As a principal at Cannon Design, he is recognized as a worldwide expert in library design and the creation of new learning environments. His projects stand in twenty-five states and more than ten countries. His design work and leadership have been recognized with an appointment to the AIA College of Fellows, the institute's highest individual honor. He is likely the last AIA Fellow without a college degree.

Stephen did all this before 1986, before you had to have a degree to become an architect. He may well be one of the last architects in a senior leadership position without a degree. Although Stephen never went through formal higher education, what's funny is that his architecture practice is largely in the education realm. He designs libraries, schools, and other new learning environments, using life experience as inspiration.

Stephen's path is not a unique one. He figured out what he was good at by trying lots of things. Some worked better than others—he never did finish that book he started in Greece—but learning what you aren't good at can be just as valuable as finding your talents. Stephen didn't know he wanted to be an architect when he came back to the office that Monday morning. He didn't know what being an architect involved. All he knew was that it would be a new experience.

If you think you're bad at music, join a choir. If you don't know anything about art, visit a museum. Join a campus group that doesn't interest you at first. Sit down for lunch in the cafeteria with people you have never met. If you think you hate traveling, buy a one-way plane ticket somewhere. It's these kinds of experiences that give you tremendous confidence—to believe you can try new things and even succeed at them. You've done something you never thought you would do or learned something you never thought you would learn. Don't ask yourself why you should try something new, ask yourself why you *shouldn't*.

Another great way to find new experiences and opportunities is through volunteering. After all, who's going to say no to free help? With the experience you gain by volunteering, you can learn the skills required to get an actual paying job.

Frank Catalano is now a successful independent consultant, but he had a long and illustrious career at traditional corporations as well as Pearson, the largest educational company in the world. But becoming the senior vice president of marketing for a billion-dollar company didn't require a college degree for Frank.

Frank got his start, of all places, by volunteering at a nearby college radio station. A high-achieving college student, Frank went to Harvey Mudd, destined to be an engineer. The son of immigrants, going to college was part of the American dream. But it wasn't part of Frank's dream.

"I recall very well when I made the decision to drop out." Frank told me, "I was in the commons, reading an assignment in *Western Man and the Environment*. I read the same page several times, not understanding what the author was trying to say. I slammed the book shut, realizing I knew what I was passionate about and the likely career path, walked to the registrar's office, and withdrew from all my courses. That same week I told the radio station I could take any paid fill-in shifts they had so that I could pay the bills."

With the skills Frank had gained from working at the college radio station, he got a real job working part-time at local radio station with a Top 40 DJ. Frank admitted that he "did weakly try to work toward a degree by enrolling later in some classes at Santa Barbara Community College while working in radio," but he decided quickly that he was doing what he loved—broadcasting—and the bills were getting paid. A few months later Frank got his first full-time job in radio and didn't look back.

In the mid-1970s, when Frank went to college, broadcast journalism degrees were rare. Experience, though volunteer, part-time, or internship work, was what radio stations were looking for. When Frank got his first radio job, the station manager told him he was glad he didn't have a degree, because otherwise they'd have to "un-train you from what you learned in college so you could work in the real world." When Frank became a news director at a radio station, he discovered the same truth when hiring—that what students learned in college was not the same as how the real world worked.

After being a station manager, Frank started his own talk radio show in Seattle, offering insights on trends in technology. It aired for five years. When the station he was working at closed down, he decided to offer his services as a strategy consultant given the expertise he had developed interviewing people on the radio. The reputation he'd developed served him well, and he found his first consulting engagement at a local software company. His clients grew in size, and ten years later he was working with Fortune 500 companies like Pearson.

Today, no matter what job you're applying for, you're expected to have a degree to get past the human resources manager. But the key for Frank was working in a field that was relatively new so that stringent requirements like having degrees weren't imposed on new employees. There are still careers that are relatively new so that a degree is not actually a requirement for the job. Or better yet, there are careers that you get to create.

Jobs tend to fall into three categories: established, developing, and new. The vocations that are still developing are relatively hard to break into without formal credentials. Scientists, doctors, and engineers fall into this category. These careers may appear established, but the methods of the field are still changing. Society keeps a tight hold on the licenses that allows one to practice these careers.

However, established and new jobs are fairly easy to break into without formal training. Established professionals are people who become writers, actors, and musicians. These are skill sets that have been around for thousands of years and haven't changed. It's easy to break into these professions with formal training because the skill set required is well established. You can easily figure out what you need to do to become a writer or a musician. It's also easy to break into a new job without a degree because, well, no one offers degrees in those things. Five years ago, who knew that you could get a job in social media or community management. I don't know of any colleges offering BAs in Twitter and Facebook yet. Schools can teach only what is settled. It takes years for knowledge to become part of a formal curriculum.

For those who have absolutely no idea of their interests, a four-year institution is a waste of money and time. Community college, a year off to explore interests, or a year to volunteer will more likely make any eventual college fruitful, if it turns out to be needed at all.

HACK OF THE DAY ||||||||||||||||||||||||||

Volunteering

Most people think of volunteering for nonprofit organizations. What you may not realize is that you can volunteer pretty much anywhere. You'll find that few people turn down the offer of free help.

1. Make a list of ten jobs that interest you. These don't need to be in the same field; it's perfectly OK if you have chemist and pastry chef on the same list.

2. For each of those ten jobs, identify someone you know who may know someone in that profession. You can ask your friends, your parents, or your professors. If you still can't find someone, post a status update on Facebook or Twitter asking if anyone knows anyone who works as a _____.

3. Through your network, build a list of people who work in the jobs that interest you.

4. Send each person an email offering to volunteer. Here is a sample email:

Hi _____,

I'm looking to learn more about being a veterinarian, but I don't know much about the day-to-day responsibilities of the job. I would like to volunteer in your office for 10 hours per week to see what it takes to be a veterinarian.

If this is an arrangement you might be interested in, let me take you out for coffee to convince you why you should let me volunteer.

Thank you,

Dale

|||||||||||||||||||||||||||||||||||||||||||||||||||||||||||||||||||||||||||||||||||||||||||||||||||||||||||||||

KNOW YOU'RE AWESOME

Derrick Carter is a world-renowned disk jockey who never finished college. He first found popularity in the Chicago house scene in the 1980s and 1990s and continues to tour around the world. I asked Derrick if there's anything that has set him apart, and without hesitation he responded, "Yeah, I think I'm awesome."

His willingness to express his self-confidence struck me, and I realized it's a common thread I've seen with people I've interviewed for this book. Many of the people I've spoken to managed to hack their education because they were self-confident. They didn't ask permission. They just started doing.

Derrick didn't sweat it when he was asked not to return to the University of Illinois. He loved learning, but he "didn't particularly care much for the institutionalized, overly rigid, and outdated way of learning." Instead, he let his awesomeness propel him.

When Derrick left school, his parents gave him an ultimatum: Go back to school, get a job, or join the army, otherwise we'll kick you out of the house. Because Derrick liked music and had been DJing events since his teens, he got a job at a record store. That source of income enabled him to move out of his parents' house and get his own DJ equipment.

Derrick started at the bottom of the DJ chain, working dances at local recreation centers, birthday parties, family reunions, and weddings. The work was nothing glamorous, but it paid the bills, and Derrick loved what he was doing.

He had a bunch of friends who lived in lofts and industrial spaces who often couldn't pay their bills. To avoid missing payments, they would throw rent parties and invite Derrick to DJ. They'd get a few kegs in the kitchen, charge $5 for a cup at the door, and the dancing followed. Derrick made a name in the loft-party scene, and then he began getting invites to play in actual clubs from promoters who had heard him at the parties. Eventually he got a residency in a club, and from there his career exploded.

Derrick's self-confidence enabled him to make the jump from playing birthday parties to flying around the world. Someone else, someone who didn't believe in himself, might have said, no, I'm not good enough to play loft parties. But Derrick said yes. And when he was invited to play in clubs again, he jumped at the opportunity and said yes. Again and again, his cockiness has enabled him to take the next step in his career.

Today, Derrick has pretty much reached the pinnacle. He tells me that he wanted to be able to travel the world and be loved for his talents, and he's done that. That's good enough he thinks.

Before I finished the interview, Derrick circled back to the question I asked initially. He wanted to make sure that I knew what he meant when he said, "I'm awesome," and didn't just think he was being a prick.

"For the most part, you can't intimidate me, and that's because I know who I am and I know what I am and I'm good with that, and there's nothing that anyone can take from me—I have to give you that power." Derrick said, "You can't take that power from me. . . . You also have to have the, I'll say balls, but there's probably a better literary word that I'll leave to your discretion to substitute, [to] just get in there and do it . . . just do it." Whenever Derrick said "do it," he jumped a little out of his seat.

If you'd don't jump out of your seat, the system will continue to whack you down. You may be told that the educational system is designed to encourage you and help you blossom, but it's not. It's vital to be confident enough in your abilities to know when it's OK to sprint ahead or do some slow jogging. In the end what matters is finding a pace that's right for you.

TWO INVALUABLE SKILLS

Schools today seem particularly bad at teaching two skills: writing and programming. When I speak to and consult with companies, these are the two skills that come up again and again. Companies ask continually for employees who can write, but they can't find any. Similarly the demand for technical talent, particularly where I live in San Francisco, is incredibly high. A few years ago, starting salaries were in the $80,000 to $90,000 range. Today, they are in the $120,000 to $140,000 range. With such demand for these skills, it boggles my mind that more people don't make a conscious effort to learn how to write and code.

What makes these skills more interesting is that both apply to a wide range of subjects and jobs. No matter what you're doing or where you're working, being able to write clearly and effectively will be an asset. No matter what you're doing or where you're working, knowing how to program computers, in a world that is increasingly focused on technology, will give you a head start over your peers.

I'm going to share the stories of two hackademics, one who found success by learning to write, and the other who found success by learning to code.

Adam Jackson is in charge of the global customer support team for TomTom, the Dutch maker of GPS devices. But he didn't always live in a beautiful home in New England and fly to Amsterdam in business class.

I met Adam when he lived in San Francisco and worked for a small, underfunded startup. On his meager salary, he rented a small apartment in the Tenderloin—the crime-ridden district of downtown San Francisco. Even then he found time to write about his job managing support and community management for the startup on his own website (adam-jackson.net). He never expected to get a call from

TomTom, a multinational corporation, wanting him to join their team.

Adam's path up until this point had been circuitous to say the least, but he always expected it to involve college. Even though Adam is twenty-four years old now, his parents still have two college funds reserved in his name. As Adam approached the decision of whether to go to college, friends told him it would be a waste of time. Once he finished high school, he moved out of his parents' place, and took a job at Arby's.

It doesn't sound glamorous, but it paid the bills during the day so that he could write by night. At the time, Adam was writing one of the most popular blogs about Apple products. A few months after he finished high school, he got a call from Apple asking him to oversee the opening of a new Apple store in Miami.

"When Apple called," Adam recalled, "I was literally driving a semitrailer. My second job was delivering doors to new homes. But that wasn't all I was doing. I was working during the day, and then when I got home I was busting my ass writing my blog and speaking about Apple at conferences." All that writing paid off; Adam never applied for that job at Apple. In fact, Apple never even had time to post it publicly. When it opened up, three people inside Apple suggested Adam to the HR department, completely unbeknownst to Adam.

Adam took the job at Apple and worked there for a year and half before moving to San Francisco to take a job with a startup. Just out of high school, Adam had achieved wild success working for the company of his dreams, and he'd gotten there by writing.

Six years later, his writing landed him the job at TomTom. These days, he's happy and healthy. He owns a home and car. He has a high six-figure salary that enables him to do pretty much whatever he wants. But despite leading a luxurious life, Adam still makes time to write. Two or three times a week, he publishes his writing to his blog. Recently, Adam started a new blog about beer, which he has begun to brew himself. Most people, if they lose their job, will see their life go to hell, but not Adam. If he ever decides to stop working at TomTom, my guess is that some beer company that's following his writing will snatch up his talents in a heartbeat.

HACK OF THE DAY ||||||||||||||||||||||

Learn to Write and Publish It!

One key to Adam's success has been his writing. It's a skill that he developed over many years, and a skill that would be valuable for you to learn. Through the process of writing publicly on your blog, you'll connect with a community of people who have similar interests. If you write publicly for long enough, people will begin to offer you jobs!

Here's how to get started:

1. If you don't already have a blog, create one. You can create a blog for free using Blogger (www.blogspot.com) or WordPress (www.wordpress.com).

2. Deciding what to write about can seem daunting, but it shouldn't be. Love dogs? Write about dogs. Are you gluten free? Write about your experiences. Interested in media? Write about the

inaccuracies you see on television. The exact topic of what you write about is irrelevant; it just needs to be something that is truly interesting to you because you're going to be writing about it a lot. And, if you write about it well, you'll be surprised at the connections and opportunities you'll make.

3. Find an editing buddy with whom you can exchange writing. Let her give you feedback and vice versa. She should be able to help catch typos in your blog posts. Unedited blog posts just look unprofessional.

4. Set writing goals for yourself. At least five hundred words per day is a good start. Set a goal of publishing your writing two to three times per week.

5. Publish your writing to your blog and share it with your friends on Facebook and Twitter. Ask your friends for feedback.

6. For specific advice on how to become a better writer, see www.uncollege.org/writing. We've compiled a list of the best online resources to help you learn to write clearly and effectively.

||||||||||||||||||||||||||||||||||||||||||||||||||||||||||||||||||||||||||||||||||||||||||||||||||||||||||||||||||||

Writing is a valuable skill, but one could argue that learning to write code is even more valuable. It is notoriously hard for English majors to find jobs, but in Silicon Valley salaries for computer engineers are about $120,000.

At twenty-three, Justin Waldron is the youngest cofounder of Zynga, the maker of Farmville and the world's largest online gaming company. It's now been four and a half years since Justin left the University of Connecticut to pursue full-time work at Zynga, but he told me it was only after Zynga's $9 billion IPO that his family stopped asking him if he ever planned on going back to school. Chances are that if you've used Facebook you've played one of the games Justin had a hand in making.

The opportunity to cofound one of the most successful online media companies came because of Justin's knowledge of computer programming. He started programming when he was eleven, and by age thirteen, he was running a website development business. By the time he got to college, the content taught in the computer science classes was information Justin had learned five years before. Boredom ensued.

Instead of doing work for his courses, Justin spent his time building online projects. Among the notches on his belt are successfully hacking AOL and having Burger King threaten to sue him because he created a website that automatically generated sandwich coupon codes. On summer vacation, Mark Pincus, now the CEO of Zynga, noticed some of Justin's projects and approached him about building online Facebook games.

By the end of the summer, the game Justin built had ten thousand daily users and was generating revenue. At that point, Justin made the decision to move to San Francisco and start Zynga instead of returning to college for his sophomore year. While the gaming market wasn't new in 2007, at the time Justin left school, it was fragmented. People spent more time online playing games than doing anything else, but no company dominated that market on the Internet until Zynga came along.

Now that Justin has been out of school for nearly five years he's starting to see his friends graduate from college. Job prospects for recent grads are few and far between because there are too many degrees and not enough job openings. There is, however, demand for certain skill sets, like computer programming, but just having a bachelor's degree doesn't do it anymore. More often than not, just getting a degree in computer science doesn't qualify you to work at a hot tech company like Zynga or Facebook or Google. Instead, hiring managers want to see experience.

HACK OF THE DAY |||||||||||||||||||||||

Learn to Code

Computer programming is a field that gives you leverage: You can build things people will use, and it scales. With relatively little effort, you can build projects that thousands or millions of people use. By no means does this mean that *everyone* should learn to code, but as we increasingly live in a world dominated by technology, learning how to interact with computers will become an increasingly useful skill. Even if you don't want to fully learn to program, make an effort to understand how programming works.

1. There are dozens of free resources on the Internet to help you learn to code. Stanford, MIT, and other schools offer their intro to computer science courses free on the Internet complete with problem sets and answers. You can gain a basic understanding through online tutorials like those found at Codecademy (www .codecademy.com). We keep a comprehensive list of resources at www.uncollege.org/code.

2. If you want to delve deeper, sign up for an intensive training program like Dev Bootcamp, or join a company like Groupon or IGN that will help you learn to code as an apprentice. Links and more are at www.uncollege.org/code.

|||||||||||||||||||||||||||||||||||||||||||||||||||||||||||||||||||||||||||||||||||||||||||||||||||||||||||||||||||||||||||||

CHAPTER FOUR

Finding Mentors and Teachers

When you teach a child something you take away forever his
chance of discovering it for himself.

—JEAN PIAGET

WHEN ANNIE WANG, THE CHIEF PRODUCT OFFICER OF THE WEBSITE HER
Campus (hercampus.com), was building the site, going to networking events on the Harvard campus directly contributed to its success.

And Her Campus has received some major recognition. *Business
Week* and *INC* have listed the team as some of the best young entrepreneurs, and Annie herself was recognized by *Forbes* as an all-star
college entrepreneur.

Some of that success comes from lessons Annie learned outside
the classroom. When Annie left Harvard, after her junior year, Her
Campus had already been in operation for nine months. "It was
simply a matter of weighing opportunity cost," Annie told me. "I
didn't feel like I could wait any longer. I knew something big was
going to happen. School was always going to be there." And because
Harvard has indefinite leaves of absences—once you're a Harvard

student you can literally return whenever you want—there was little risk.

Mentors, advisers, and friends of Her Campus have been crucial to its success. Annie casually drops names of Her Campus's advisers: "People like Will Schenck have become mentors and we were able to personally meet Arianna Huffington by going to events at Harvard," she said. Will Schenck is the former editor of *Rolling Stone*. Arianna Huffington is the founder of the *Huffington Post* and editorial czar at AOL. Those are two pretty awesome people to have on your side.

The Her Campus team met Will and Arianna by going to events at Harvard. They went to events that relevant people were attending and just went up and had a conversation with them afterward. They took the initiative to start a dialogue and simply start talking with the speaker. Her Campus has now been going for three years, and it's cash-flow positive. Annie is making bank. Although she never took any computer science courses at Harvard, Annie is now the CPO. She built the entire website from scratch without any formal training.

She started by learning online; again she chose to use the resources of the university. She figured out that you can go to lectures in the computer science department, go to office hours, and even reach out to alumni for mentorship. You just have to take the initiative. Universities are awesome resources. Use them.

Attend Lectures on a College Campus

Just as Annie and the Her Campus team went to events at Harvard, you can go to events at a college campus near you whether or not you're a student. No one is going to check if you're a current student. Here's how:

1. Identify a university campus near you, the bigger the better because larger campuses have more events. If you're totally lost, use CollegeBoard (www.collegeboard.com).
2. Choose a week, and go to every event humanly possible that week. Go to events that interest you. Attend lectures, film screenings, and movie recitals.
3. After each event, introduce yourself to the presenter. Ask for his contact information and follow up by email afterward.

||||||||||||||||||||||||||||||||||||||||||||||||||||||||||||||||||||||||||||||||||||||||||||||||||||

REACHING OUT TO MENTORS

Laura Deming's mentors have had a profound impact on her life. They were the biggest reason she found herself at MIT as a freshman when she was fourteen years old. They were the same reason she started working in labs when she was twelve. Laura's mentors didn't come from her parents' connections. She found them herself.

Laura was a naturally curious child—like all children are—and spent hours researching subjects she loved. She's thankful she never went to school, because her naïveté allowed her to believe she could do anything. "When you're a kid you have no idea what's out there," she told me, "and to some extent we still don't know. But as a kid you think you're invincible." That sense of invincibility led Laura to pursue her passions, to explore, and to create. She stumbled upon biology and was mesmerized. As she described her vivid recollection of the first biological steps she became serious: "The first thing that got me interested in biology was playing with a model of DNA. I was so excited by this massive model of balls and strands I couldn't put it down. Learning that these little things controlled who we are—and who we become—was amazing."

Over the course of the next few years, Laura continued to explore the impact of biology. She started looking into cancer researching, diabetes research, and she delved deeper and discovered antiaging research. Laura described it as "the holy grail of biology." She loved it because it was where she could have the most impact.

So Laura started emailing leading scientists who work on antiaging research. One of the experts she emailed, Cynthia Kenyon, responded. Cynthia's lab at the University of California at San Francisco (UCSF) did pioneering work in the field—she discovered in 1993 that a single gene alteration in a worm could double its life span. Laura emailed Cynthia to ask if she could tour her lab.

Laura was twelve. She didn't ask for an internship or a job. All she asked Cynthia was if she could come tour the facility. And Cynthia said yes.

So Laura visited the lab. After her visit, Laura emailed Cynthia asking if she could work in the lab, doing anything that needed to be done. Cynthia, a wonderful mentor and enthusiastic scientist, was willing to let Laura run experiments in the lab. Laura was ecstatic.

Laura got to laser worms, gape at glowing images of fluorescent nematodes, make the critters live six times longer than normal, and learn from erudite grad students. But after a few years, Laura felt the need to see what college was like. She wanted to go to a place filled with scientists and engineers, people passionate about the subject she loved. She had seen MIT as that place since she was ten, so she decided to apply early to MIT. She did, and she was accepted.

"If you want to find a mentor," Laura said to me, "you've got to email the leading lights in the field that you're interested in. Don't bother working your way up from the bottom. Go straight to the top. People will respond. Unless you take that first step, no one is going to hand you an opportunity."

Today, at seventeen, Laura, like me, is a member of the inaugural class of Thiel Fellows, working on finding solutions to end aging and enable everyone to live happier and healthier lives. When I asked Laura how she found the email addresses of experts such as Cynthia Kenyon, she gave me a look as if I'd asked the world's most stupid question. "I Google them. It's not difficult," she told me. "The difficult part is having the guts to send someone a cold email."

Laura also introduced me to Christian Keller. Christian left school in Switzerland when he was thirteen. He didn't even ask his parents' permission; he just sent his school a letter saying he would no longer be attending. After that, Christian found a local high school that allowed him to take the final exams without completing the course-work. He took them, he passed, and he got his high school diploma.

Now twenty-five, Christian has spent the last seven years of his life working on a film in Mexico called *Gloria* that is based on the life of a punk/rock star from the 1980s of the same name. Christian heard about her story, thought it would make a good film, but didn't know where to start. He decided to email a famous movie producer, Barrie Osbourne, who won an Oscar for producing *The Lord of the Rings* and is known for his work on *The Matrix* as well.

Christian didn't have Barrie's email address, so he just started guessing, trying different combinations of Barrie's name at his company's domain. It took a few tries, but eventually he found the correct address, and Barrie responded. A few days later, Christian traveled to meet Barrie at his home to convince him to work on the film. Barrie agreed, and today they're working together on *Gloria*, with Christian directing and Barrie producing. They just closed a $9 million round of funding for the film and will begin shooting in early 2013. If all goes well, the film will be in theaters that December.

If you want to get in touch with someone whose email address is unlisted, here are some basic strategies for guessing the address. There are two parts to guessing someone's email address: the username and the domain name. The username is the part before the at symbol (@). This is the easiest to guess as the combinations are often standardized. If you wanted to email me, and assuming my name is Dale Stephens, some combinations to try would be these:

1. DaleS@uncollege.org
2. DaleStephens@uncollege.org

3. Dale@uncollege.org

4. DStephens@uncollege.org

Googling "Dale Stephens" should give you a good idea of what domain names you should email. UnCollege.org is obvious. DaleStephens.com would be another. If you see that I'm part of the Thiel Fellowship you could try emailing me at something like DaleStephens@thielfellowship.org. You can repeat this process to guess anyone's email. It takes chutzpah and persistence, but as Christian's story shows, the rewards can be tremendous.

HACK OF THE DAY ||||||||||||||||||||||||||

Reach Out to an Expert

If you aren't enrolled in college, you can easily seek mentorship, guidance, and advice from professors. Office hours are open to anyone, not just students. If you're genuinely interested in learning, professors are often happy to share their knowledge, no matter if you're a student or not. Universities post public directories of their faculty on their websites, so you can easily find email addresses and sometimes even phone numbers. I know there is a subject that you'd love to learn more about. Is it biology? English? History? Math? Whatever it is, chances are that your local university has someone that knows about it.

1. Identify the subject for which you want to speak to an expert.

2. Find a local university. CollegeBoard (www.collegeboard.com) has a nice directory if you don't already know one close to home.

3. Browse the university's website by department, looking for the likely experts. Sometimes this is easy: Math people are in the math department. Other times this can take more sleuthing: For example, statistics experts might be in a social science department.

4. Once you've found that person, find her email address. If not already listed on the department web page, universities have a "people search" function that you can access from the home page.

5. Send your potential mentor an email. The key to sending such an email is twofold:

Ask for a very short amount of time.

Ask for something very specific.

||||||||||||||||||||||||||||||||||||||||||||||||||||||||||||||||||||||||||||||||||||||||||||||||||||||||||||||||||||

HOW HACKADEMICS WRITE EMAILS

It can be really frustrating to send email to potential mentors, companies, or anyone you want to connect with and get no response. It doesn't make sense: Email takes only take a few minutes to compose, so shouldn't the response also take only a few minutes?

I used to think the same thing. Now I get more email than I know what to do with. However, it is significantly easier to respond if people follow some basic rules. Don't think of these as *rules*; rather think of them as ways to get my attention. The best emails are concise. They are no more than two or three sentences and spell out a specific request. As much as your life story is interesting, not everyone has time to read it. An email such as this is highly effective:

Hi Dale

I was unschooled like you, and would love to chat for 30 minutes on Tuesday the 14th at 12pm at Tartine on Guerrero Street about XYZ.

This person piqued my interest by telling me he was unschooled and made a very specific request. He requested a coffee meeting about a specific topic and suggested a specific time and place. This is crucial. I can respond to this from my iPhone saying, "Sure, are you free tomorrow at 2pm?"

Hacking the email subject line is the best way to get people to respond to your email quickly. If you're being introduced to someone via a third party, put that person's name in the subject line. But even if you're not working off of an introduction you can still write effective email subject lines. If you're following up with a new business contact, put your name, company, or school and phone number in the subject line. This makes it super easy to add you into contacts. Here are examples of real email subject lines I have received:

Will you be my mentor?
→ This email subject contains a direct question. The body of this email contained a few sentences on why I should mentor the sender of the email. She was persuasive, and I said yes.

Enormous idea

→ This is not helpful whatsoever. I have no idea what the idea is, let alone whether it is in fact enormous. This email is automatically sorted into a folder labeled "later." The sad reality is that later often never comes.

Introduction from Jon Bischke

→ This is effective because I know Jon and trust his recommendations. If you were recommended to contact someone by a third party, always put his or her name in the subject line. It will make the recipient more likely to open your email.

I'm a CEO dropout

→ I opened this email because this person has been successful without a college degree. I'm interested in those people.

Anderson Cooper

→ Putting the name of a famous person in the subject line also gets people to open email. In this case, the email was an interview request from Anderson Cooper's show.

Good morning, Dale

→ This is useless. The person has no idea when I will get this email. Again, this goes in the "later" folder.

A quick question for you

→ If you have a question, ask it in the subject line. Write the question directly in the subject line, like this: "Are you free for coffee on Tuesday?"

FROM EMAIL TO COFFEE

Exchanging emails with a mentor or teacher is wonderful, but to make the relationship more meaningful, I suggest you take it offline. Email is a wonderful tool, but it's not the same as engaging in a real conversation with someone.

When I first moved to San Francisco and began to find mentors in the technology and entrepreneurship world, I started by emailing people I admired and offering to buy them coffee. Many accepted, and for this purpose I specifically budgeted $150 per month to buy coffee for people I wanted to learn from. It's the least I could do to compensate for their time.

At a high estimate, if each cup of coffee costs $3, I could afford to have thirty interesting conversations per month—one per day! And that I did. For the first few months I lived in San Francisco I made sure I bought one person coffee every single day. Many of the people I bought coffee for have become ardent friends and supporters. Buying coffee was a sound investment.

A few thousand miles away, at Michigan State University, an under-graduate student named Megan Gebhart was also buying people coffee. In July 2010, Megan decided she would drink fifty-two cups of coffee over the course of the following year. But not just any cup of coffee; another person had to be present, and it couldn't be someone that she typically would have coffee with. Not only did she drink coffee, she spent time writing about what she learned along the way, and posted essays after each cup at *52 Cups of Coffee* (www.52cups .tumblr.com).

Two years before, Megan had learned how a single cup of coffee could change her life. A mutual friend had introduced her to another student, Brett, and suggested they meet for coffee. "We had a lot in common" Megan said. "We both had an entrepreneurial mind-set, liked helping people, and wanted to connect with other like-minded students."

The two became fast friends. Since that time, Brett has introduced Megan to a wide variety of people, taught her numerous things, helped her with various projects, opened doors to new opportunities, and—most important—been a fantastic friend.

Megan couldn't help but wonder what would happen if she made it a habit to meet new people. Obviously every meeting wouldn't lead to the same outcome as that fateful cup of coffee with Brett, but when you invite fifty-two new people into your life, it's bound to change somehow.

So Megan spent an entire year having coffee with—and thereby developed relationships with—people that she never would have met otherwise. The journey took her from Warsaw, Poland, to New York City to the middle of Wyoming. Over the course of the year, she had coffee with everyone from a six-year-old Native American to bestselling author Seth Godin to cofounder of Apple Steve Wozniak.

"College taught me how to make a living, but *52 Cups* taught me how to live," Megan told me.

It's clear that the project has been truly life changing for Megan. Over the course of a year and seven countries, Megan was able to see the world from fifty-two new perspectives. She learned lessons from real life instead of lessons out of a textbook and met incredible people along the way. You can read about Megan's journey and what she learned in the process at *52 Cups of Coffee*.

These days, now that I've found an extensive network of mentors and teachers, I don't drink nearly as much coffee. Somehow I now find myself on the other end of this equation—people are now emailing me asking if they can take me out for coffee. If I'm at home, I always try to say yes. Having coffee takes only thirty minutes. The worst possible outcome is that I'll spend thirty minutes learning about someone else. That's not so bad. The best possible outcome is that I'll make a new friend, maybe even find a new mentor or teacher. With coffee meetings you never know what the outcome will be. The only way to find out is to try.

HACK OF THE DAY

Take People Out for Coffee

Not only is having coffee a great way to meet people and build your network, it can teach you a lot about not caring what people think. You'll eventually realize you can have an open conversation about anything. You'll learn that even a huge pimple or bad hair day won't impede your ability to connect with strangers.

1. Invite someone you don't know very well to have coffee. During your conversation, explain that you're taking one person to coffee every week for a year. Ask him whom else you should meet.
2. Have a second cup of coffee, and repeat the process. Get a suggestion for cup number three from cup number two.

3. Repeat.
4. Write about your experiences publicly like Megan did. Start a blog and tell the world about your journey.

||||||||||||||||||||||||||||||||||||||||||||||||||||||||||||||||||||||||||||||||||||||||||||||||||||||||||||||||

BECOME AN APPRENTICE

In Germany to become an aircraft mechanic or hotel manager you don't go to a university. Instead, you enter into an apprenticeship program where you learn largely through on-the-job training. The multiplicity of ways to enter the workforce in Germany—through both apprenticeships and universities—means that Germany has one of the lowest youth unemployment rates in all of Europe. In Germany, only 7.8 percent of German youths are unemployed.[1] However, this is not to say that the German system is perfect. Homeschooling is illegal in Germany, and kids are tracked into the different systems at a very young age. While I don't think either of these things is good, we can learn from the apprenticeship system.

Apprenticeships are slowly making a resurgence in the United States. Siemens, the German engineering firm, recently reported that they would be bringing back welding apprentices to make up for a jobs shortage in their U.S. factories. Groupon, the online retailer, runs an apprenticeship program to help nontraditional learners learn how to code. In 2011, IGN, the online gaming site, started a six-week mini apprenticeship program to screen new talent; the program was a wild success, and its second iteration is under way.

It's going to be a while before apprenticeship programs are established at major corporations, so some people like Ryan Holiday have chosen to become an apprentice to an individual.

At just twenty-four, Ryan is the director of marketing for American Apparel and a highly paid brand and strategy consultant to authors and Fortune 500 companies. To get where he is today he started as an apprentice.

Ryan likes saying yes to absurd things. One of the most pivotal was saying, "Fuck it, yes—I'm going to live on Tucker Max's floor instead of going to college and become a research assistant."

Back when Ryan decided to live with Tucker, Tucker wasn't famous. He was just a guy blogging about his illustrious sexual encounters at TuckerMax.com. Ryan is the marketing genius behind Tucker's story—and part of the reason Tucker's first book, *I Hope They Serve Beer in Hell*, spent five years on the *New York Time*'s bestseller list and sold over 1 million copies in print. By any measure that is wild success; the average book sells only a few thousand copies.

Ryan first emailed Tucker to ask to interview him for his school newspaper when he was attending the University of California at Riverside on a full-ride Chancellor's scholarship. He was on track to graduate in just three years, but after emailing Tucker, Ryan began doing part-time work for him. At the end of his second year, Ryan moved to Los Angeles to work for Tucker, initially living on his floor. Ryan assumed he would return to school but that never happened. Ryan dropped out.

But working with Tucker wasn't the only thing Ryan did that summer; he also worked with a movie producer and talent manager to design a strategy for the band Linkin Park. "My mentor there told me it would drive me crazy to go back to school and read in the news about the projects I put in motion and the people I worked with," Ryan recalled. The week Ryan decided he was going to drop out, he had lunch with Tucker and his friend Robert Greene. Robert was complaining that he needed a research apprentice for his next book, and Ryan volunteered.

Through working for Robert, Ryan met Dov Charney, a fellow college dropout and founder of American Apparel. "It was just like college," Ryan told me. "In college you take chemistry and philosophy and math and literature. Instead, I was taking Dov Charney, Robert Greene, Tucker Max, and Linkin Park."

Ryan always wanted to be a writer, and now he is—in fact, a bestselling one. Penguin published his first book, *Trust Me, I'm Lying: Confessions of a Media Manipulator*, in 2012 to an advance of more than $250,000. Ryan tells me he doesn't need the money. Now, it doesn't seem like that much to him, but looking back it does. When he dropped out of college he earned $30,000 his first year as a research apprentice.

Work as a research apprentice wasn't always glamorous, but it afforded unlimited opportunities for learning. More important, becoming a research apprentice was a direct catapult into the media world that Ryan wanted to be a part of. Working as an apprentice for an individual means you have a lot more influence and responsibility than you ever would if you decided to take an internship at some big company like Google. Most important, if you do your job well, you'll develop a relationship with the person you're working for that will last a lifetime. Having influential people batting for your team is always a good thing.

Become an Apprentice

Tucker Max wrote an incredible blog post about the process of hiring his most recent research assistant. You can read the entire post (which is a few thousand words long) at *TuckerMax. Me*,[2] but I'm going to summarize a few of the most salient points here:

1. Identify someone who you would like to be an apprentice for. Start by looking at the authors of books in the field that interests you. Make a list of ten people for whom you would like to apprentice.

2. Email each of those people and offer to do something for free. These people all have things they'd like done but don't have the time to do. Tucker's example is to transcribe podcasts for free and email them to the creator, but that's just one example. You could compile a list of conferences that person might want to speak at. You could write thoughtful responses to blog comments.

3. Although you're not getting paid, you are working for this person. If you're helpful enough, she'll take notice and realize that you're so helpful she should hire you.

4. Another of Tucker's previous assistants, Charlie Hoehn, wrote a thirty-page e-book on getting hired by doing free work.*

---

* Charlie Hoehn, "Announcing: My First e-Book," *Hoehn's Musings*, July 14, 2009, http://charliehoehn.com/2009/07/14/announcing-my-first-e-book.

|||||||||||||||||||||||||||||||||||||||||||||||||||||||||||||||||||||||||||||||||||||||||||||||||||

LEARN FROM YOUR PEERS

Traditionally we think of being an intern or apprentice for someone who is older, wiser, and more experienced than ourselves. But what if that assumption weren't true? What if we could learn just as much from each other as from a professor or expert?

When I was an unschooler, my collaborative learning groups frequently involved learning from our peers. Sometimes we'd take turns presenting on preassigned topics to the group—say one person would present about Greece in the year 1000 while another would present about Rome—and other times we'd simply share our knowledge collaboratively. For example, we had a math group that met on Tuesday afternoon at which a math professor would help the kids who were learning calculus, the kids learning calc would help the kids learning trig, the kids learning trig would help the kids learning algebra, and so forth.

Many of my unschooling peers during sixth to twelfth grades had parents who were professors at a university, a pretty well-known university, in fact: the University of California at Davis. Although those parents were invested in the system, they knew that the school system wouldn't provide the best education for their children. They wanted their kids to be able to engage in the same type of experiential learning as their graduate students did.

So instead of trying to work around the system, they pulled their kids out of school. Children and parents collaborated to organize cooperative learning groups, often rotating living rooms so an expert in a particular subject was present to facilitate discussions. Although my parents don't have PhDs, when I left school I was invited to participate in this academic ecosystem. I learned collaboratively with my friends and sought out guidance from experts.

My school experience was not that of a homeschooler; I did not sit at home in my pajamas all day doing dittos. Instead, I created a school environment from the world around me. I didn't spend much time at home, and what I was doing didn't look much like school. The academic classes that we organized were called *cooperatives* because we all worked together in planning the curriculum.

For all of our learning groups, online learning resources were invaluable. In the early 2000s, Khan Academy didn't exist, but what did exist was the Massachusetts Institute of Technology Open-CourseWare platform, an initiative to put all the learning materials from MIT courses online, for free. Launched in 2002, the project uses Creative Commons licenses to enable people to share and distribute the content freely.

Joi Ito has long been a proponent of open-source philosophy and is today the chairman of Creative Commons as well as a director of the well-known Media Lab at MIT. Even though Joi now works for MIT, he didn't drop out of college just once but twice: first from Tufts University and later from the University of Chicago.

Joi was bored in school and felt that he was learning more about computer networking by actually using computers rather than sitting in classes. Because he didn't want to spend his days listening to lectures, he dropped out of Tufts and moved to Chicago to pursue a career as a disk jockey.

Joi has spent much of his life involved in technology and computing. Today, he's an active investor in companies like Twitter and Kickstarter, and on the board of organizations like Mozilla and ICANN. The Internet has forever changed how we learn. The Internet allows you to find information when you need it. You find resources as you need them; you just need to know where to look and who to ask. But skills such as how to find resources are not taught in college.

"Most of college education is about what you can do on your own, without cheating," Joi told me. "But cheating involves really important skills—such as how to find the answer from somebody else and how to take shortcuts." Instead of sitting in college learning, these skills, most people are sitting in college fulfilling requirements for graduation.

The Internet is one of the best learning tools out there because you can customize your own experience. You can find information on just about anyone or anything. You can publish blog posts. You can create YouTube videos. You can even create massive communities of people who teach each other.

Peer-to-peer teaching already exists in many communities; that's how computer programmers teach each other, and that's how writers give and get feedback on their work. That's partly why the content quality on Wikipedia is so good (and often more accurate than the major print encyclopedias). The Wikipedia community is a really interesting community of people working together on teaching each other how to think. In video games—like World of Warcraft or Pokémon or Yu-Gi-Oh—you see people teaching each other.

"If you just look at the forum sites for video games, even World of Warcraft, there's a lot of math going on," Joi told me. "There's a website called Elitist Jerks, where all of the really, really hard-core gamers talk about statistics and spells and stuff like that. But that's some really serious math."

If you can teach others about Pokémon, you can use the same methodology to teach each other about differential equations, American history, or covalent chemical bonds. The subject matter is irrelevant. What matters is that you understand the mind-set that's required to learn from your peers. You have to assume that everyone around you is smart. That everyone around you has something to share. That everyone around you is capable of teaching. Even you can be a teacher.

HACK OF THE DAY

Teach Your Friends Something You Know

We all have hidden talents, and it's time we shared them with the world. Your challenge today is to invite your friends over to help them learn something from you to practice peer-to-peer teaching.

1. Decide what you're going to help your friends learn. Will you teach them how to cook Indian food? Do online marketing? Identify weeds in a garden? We all have a skill to share—don't be shy.

2. Invite three to eight friends over for one hour to learn a new skill. If you're feeling audacious, make the learning group public at E-180 (www.e-180.com) or Skillshare (www.skillshare.com).

3. After you share your knowledge with your friends, reflect on the experience. Do you feel more knowledgeable now? What did you learn about yourself in the process of teaching?

CHAPTER FIVE

Building a Community/Network

If you want to get laid, go to college. If you want an education,
go to the library.
—FRANK ZAPPA

WHEN I ANNOUNCED I WAS LEAVING COLLEGE AND MOVING BACK TO SAN
Francisco, the responses from my friends and peers fell into two
broad categories. My friends from college usually offered something
like condolences, often tinged with confusion. "I'm sorry to see you
go," was the usual refrain across my Facebook wall.

But among those were also responses from my friends and col-
leagues from San Francisco. Their responses almost invariably used
the word *congrats* and often included offers of jobs or couches to
crash on while I got myself set up.

Seeing this burst of support is when I first truly understood the
importance of building a community—people whom you truly love
and who share your values. As we bring new people into our community, we share those values with them and learn from their experiences. Having these connections can be the difference between not

making it at all and making it big. By the end of this chapter you'll know how to bring smart and talented people into your professional network and also how to make some of those people part of your personal community.

When I moved to San Francisco in the spring of 2010, I had no community and no network. I got my first job at Zinch—a company that helps people get into college—by reaching out to the founder, Mick Hagen, on Twitter. Even though these days I'm doing more to help people get out of college, Mick and I are still friends. In fact, without Mick I probably wouldn't be writing this book. He has served as an amazing mentor and example to me as I've navigated my own life. He gave me my first job, and was the first guy to encourage me not to go to college. He introduced me to dozens of people who became part of my network and later part of my community.

DROPPING OUT AND HELPING PEOPLE GET INTO COLLEGE

Mick is a college dropout himself. And at the time he left Princeton, Zinch was only an idea. There was no code base, designs, or even pitch deck. It was just an inkling of an idea. After leaving, Mick moved home to Utah, founded Zinch with his brother and a friend, and set up shop in Provo.

With his cofounders, he built a working website. They went through many product iterations and, after talking with college admission offices for many months, finally had a product schools wanted to use. They let the first few schools try the product for free, with the understanding that if they liked it they would pay for it in a few months. After a few months of testing, they signed their first college as a client.

The future looked bright, and they began hiring engineers to build a new version of the website and salespeople to bring on more universities as clients. Before he knew it, Mick had ten employees and Zinch was running out of money. He'd gotten ahead of himself. "We needed to raise money quickly or the company was going to fold," he told me.

But Mick had a problem: He didn't know any investors. "In Utah, there is a foundation that gives out awards to the top hundred best entrepreneurs in Utah—the V100," Mick told me. "We figured that since we were entrepreneurs from Utah we could make connections and learn from some of these people. We thought they could be mentors to us. We tracked down the contact information for one hundred entrepreneurs and emailed them or called them until we got a response." Mick met with nearly all one hundred entrepreneurs from the list—there were only two or three whom he couldn't reach. At the end of this process, Mick had added almost a hundred new people to his network.

That persistence led Mick to an introduction to the man who would become Zinch's lead investor, Mike Levinthal. Mike had invested in some of the entrepreneurs Mick had met, and those entrepreneurs offered to introduce Mick to him.

But it wasn't until he'd met about forty people that the first person offered an introduction to Mike, and it took until Mick had met ninety people before two more people recommended Mick to Mike. Due in large part to the recommendations Mike received, he became Zinch's first investor. He made connections to other investors and convinced them to join in.

Three years later, Zinch was successfully acquired by Chegg, the textbook rental company. In between those three years was a lot of hard work. The team moved from Utah to San Francisco to be closer to Silicon Valley. As the client base got bigger they had to rebuild the site to support more traffic and higher use. This was rocky and didn't go so well with all the clients. The team worked long hours to resolve the problems and make all of its users happy. After that, the client base continued to grow, and education companies became interested in acquiring the business Chegg bought.

Although Mick is now twenty-five, he hasn't lost any of that hustle from when he was younger. His new company, Undrip, a social media filtering company, is set to launch soon and is now raising money. This time he didn't email a hundred people; he found a new tactic: rap videos. Mick is a minor YouTube dance and rap celebrity (a few of his videos have several million views) and is creating personal raps for the people he wants as investors. He's got a list of ten people—all A-list investors—and has written personalized raps and music videos detailing to each why they should invest in his company. In the end, none of the people he specifically targeted invested in Undrip, but he did get investment from people who reached out to him because they saw the videos. In other words, Mick would have never connected with the people had he not made the videos. By creating the Undrip videos, Mick created a network of people interested in his product. Some of those people he brought into his community as investors or as early users of the product. Now these people are ardent supporters of Mick.

CONFERENCE HACKING

Getting into and speaking at conferences is another perfect way to start expanding your network. Conferences are amazing opportunities to connect with like-minded individuals, learn new things, and find inspiration for your next project. They aren't hard to find—conferences happen all the time. A great directory of conferences is available at Lanyrd.com. Unfortunately, some conferences are extremely expensive—the prestigious TED conference costs $7,500—but there are ways around that. The first, and best, way to hack a conference is to speak at the conference.

Think you don't have anything to say at a conference? Think again. I bet that you, right now, can find a conference that will bring you to speak and pay your travel expenses. Most conferences want speakers who can talk about personal experiences. Do you have a food allergy? Give a speech about adversity. Part of a minority (ethnic, sexuality, socioeconomic, or otherwise)? Give a speech about finding success as that demographic. Those are just two ideas—I guarantee that you can find a conference that will want to hear you speak. If you don't want to talk about yourself but rather an idea, speak at a TEDx event. TEDx events are franchises licensed by TED—the well-known conference organized around technology, entertainment, and design every year in Long Beach, California. Hundreds—and soon probably thousands—of TEDx events take place every year. They are focused on everything from life extension to sports. You can find one to suit your interests. Even better, there are TEDxYouth and TEDxKids events—specifically targeted at having young speakers. They happen all over the world.

Pitch Yourself to a Conference

I want you to speak at a conference. To do that, you have to email a conference telling them why you should speak. Actually, you'll have to pitch yourself to twenty conferences, but once you've done one, it's really easy.

1. Go to TEDx events page (www.ted.com/tedx) and look at upcoming events. You'll find thousands. You can narrow your search by interest, but I suggest you choose where to pitch yourself based on where you want to travel. Want to go to Africa? TEDx-Soweto. India? TEDxJaipur. Germany? TEDxBerlin.

2. One you've chosen an event, email the organizer even if the event says they aren't looking for speakers. Events are always looking for more speakers. Your email should look something like this:

I lead _____ the social movement/project/company changing the notion that _____. I have been recognized as a _____. I have spoken at _____. I'm an expert in _____ because

I've been interviewed in _____ press outlets. I want to speak about _____ because my _____ experience gives me a unique perspective on _____.

Make sure to include links in your email to your personal website where you've been keeping track of your projects, goals, and accomplishments. Include any other relevant links about you as well—perhaps news articles or a profile on your university's website. You probably don't think of yourself as an expert in something; I certainly didn't when I started emailing conferences. Then I realized that we are all experts in our own experience. We all have a unique perspective on life, and that alone qualifies you as an expert.

3. This probably won't work the first time; it didn't for me. Eventually, however, someone will invite you to speak. Expect to email at least twenty conferences before someone actually invites you to give a talk.
4. If pitching yourself as a speaker doesn't work, ask if there are reduced rates for students; the people who run these conferences know you're probably strapped for cash. Some of these deals are advertised, some aren't. If there's no option for a student ticket, email the organizer making the case for why you should get a free ticket. The key here is to emphasize not only what you will learn but also what value you will add to the conference.

If that doesn't work, offer some sweat equity—say that you'll volunteer in exchange for a ticket. Many conferences have official volunteer schemes outlined on their websites, but if not, you should email the organizer anyhow.

If you can't convince a conference to give you a free ticket by volunteering, just show up. At best you'll make friends with the organizer and charm him or her into giving you a badge. At worst you can sit in the lobby, snack on free food, and meet people in between sessions.

||||||||||||||||||||||||||||||||||||||||||||||||||||||||||||||||||||||||||||||||||||||||||||||||||||||||||||||||||||||||||||

My friend Cory Levy mastered the art of conference hacking in high school. In summer 2010, Cory was on summer vacation with his family in Aspen, Colorado. On his last day there he was wandering around town and saw a bunch of brand-new Infiniti cars with signs that said "Fortune Tech Brainstorm" on them. "This looks interesting," he said to himself and promptly Googled it on his phone. He recognized a few speakers, looked at the agenda, and decided he couldn't miss the keynote. Cory dashed back to his hotel to change into nicer clothes.

After changing, Cory hopped into one of the waiting Infiniti conference cars, a convertible Infiniti G37S. Chuckling, Cory recalls what the driver asked him: "Wanna drive?" Cory let the expert stay behind the wheel.

"I showed up to the conference and jumped in the registration line," Cory told me. "After a few minutes of waiting, it was my turn in line. I stepped up and said, 'I am an eighteen-year-old entrepreneur from Houston. I am here with my family in Aspen and just found out about this conference. I Googled it, recognized a few speakers, and I was wondering if I could sit in on one session.' I was hoping to hear a 'Yes, of course!' But I heard quite the opposite: 'This is an invitational-only conference—admission is thirty-five hundred dollars. We are sorry but we cannot just let you in.'"

Cory walked outside and called a friend who had crashed events before. With his friend's advice, Cory walked back into registration and asked to speak with the head of PR. He wasn't there, but another woman who worked in PR was, so Cory gave her his website name and URL and two-minute elevator pitch like he had at the registration desk. From her language, Cory knew it wasn't looking good: "Please wait over there while I see what I can do," she said. Hoping for the best to simply sit in one session, she comes back saying, "We are sorry but the press contacts us weeks before the event; we can't just let you in the day of the event."

Cory walked out and asked the Infiniti driver for a ride back to his place. "I was talking to my driver and told him what happened," he recalled. "I asked if Infiniti, a gold sponsor of the conference, might be able to get me into one session. I called the head Infiniti guy who then gave me the email address of the head of PR for the conference. I sent an email to Daniel Kile, the head of PR, and then called his office. Someone in his office who works for him said he would flag it. No response. I sent a cold text to Scott Raymond, the founder of Gowalla. Founders Fund—a VC firm that I interned for in high school—invested in Gowalla and I had talked with Scott the previous summer. That's how I had his number. I texted him saying I worked at Founders Fund last summer. He was speaking the following morning, and I was hoping he would be able to get me in to watch his session. After a few back-and-forth texts, he told me about an after party at 10:30 p.m."

Cory showed up early to an already packed room at the after party. Scott had gone to bed early because he had an early session in the morning, so Cory didn't know anyone at the party. As he was about to walk in, Cory ran into the woman who had kicked him out earlier. She said, 'You found the after party—I'm impressed.'"

After chatting with a bunch of people, Cory ended up meeting Daniel Kile. His goal at the beginning of the day was to sit in on one session. But Cory talked his way into a conference pass and was able to attend the entire conference on Friday and Saturday. Cory had an established two-minute pitch and was persistent (in the next section I'll help you develop your own pitch). Both these qualities impressed the right people at the conference.

There are a couple things to learn from Cory's story of hacking the conference:

- **Don't take no for an answer.** Even when people told Cory what he wanted wasn't possible, he kept pushing. He got past the party-pooping PR lady in this way. Be persistent.

- **Make connections with the inside.** Even while Cory was pushing on the outside, he was emailing and texting friends on the inside. You can check Facebook, Twitter, and LinkedIn to see if anyone you know is in attendance. If not, look for people who work for the same company—maybe your uncle works at Google and someone from Google is at this conference. Ask your uncle for this person's email or phone number. This is key: Getting someone already inside to hold open a door for me has worked many a time. Note that Cory didn't personally know the people he was texting; he just cold texted them.

- **Don't be afraid to cold text, call, or email.** To write a persuasive cold text, make sure to include a reference to your mutual connection. In Cory's case, his text probably looked something like this:

> Hi Scott, I'm Cory Levy. We interacted when I worked for Founders Fund last summer. I'm in Aspen and noticed you were here for the ideas festival. I'd love to come to the after party, but I can't find it—could you share the location with me?

- **Try multiple avenues simultaneously.** Cory pursued Infiniti, friends, and the PR route all at the same time; he didn't know which would pan out so he kept his options open.

- **Dress nicely.** Looking smart always helps.

- **Make nice to the sponsors.** If the guys who are writing the checks like you, they can often help.

- **Be able to pitch yourself.** Cory had his two-minute elevator pitch down and was able to tell people exactly who he was and why he was there.

- **Don't be afraid to ask.** Cory could have just seen the signs and thought, "That's way too big for me." Instead, he marched straight up to one of the cars, hopped in, and asked for a badge. You'd be surprised how many people wouldn't even ask. It's usually quite easy to get free shit because people don't even bother asking.

Even if Cory hadn't been able to obtain a badge, he still would have been able to gain value from crashing the conference. Going badgeless is the way to go—it makes attending conferences way more fun than if you were following the rules. My finale to leaving college was going to South by Southwest, the interactive arts and technology festival in Austin, Texas. However, because I decided to go at the last minute, the conference badges were already long sold out.

This meant that I got to hack the conference. Fortunately, I had convinced Rebecca Goldman, my fellow unschooler who helped me start UnCollege, to join me—the two of us made quite a duo. We ducked and weaved our way to conference success. To make matters more entertaining, neither of us was twenty-one, nor did we have fake IDs, and the life of SxSW is at parties that are twenty-one-plus. But we didn't see this as a bad thing—it was more of a challenge.

When approaching a party we'd do a walk around the perimeter while we used our phones to see who had checked in on Foursquare. If someone we knew had checked in, we texted him to let us in the back door. If we didn't know anyone, we took to Twitter and began tweeting the people who had checked in on Foursquare. To our surprise, this worked, and we made some nice friends this way.

After we successfully sneaked into a full night of parties, we decided we had to move on to the next step: sneaking into sessions. One way to get in is to walk up to the table and take one of the leftover badges after the conference has already started. There are inevitably people who don't show up for conferences, and it is silly to waste their spot. Most conferences don't check IDs. Another thing to do is to walk up to the registration table at a conference you haven't registered for and insist that you have. If they ask for confirmation, say that you didn't print the email. Nine times out of ten they will print you a new badge. Free badge, zero cost.

Another trick for the well-prepared conference hacker is preparing your own badge in advance. As crazy as this may sound, I actually keep my own homemade conference badges in my bag at all times. It simply reads "UnCollege—Dale J. Stephens." Throw the badge on and walk into any conference or party—hardly anyone will notice if it's not exactly the right color.

HACKING PERSONAL INTRODUCTIONS

So you've hacked your way into a conference, either as a participant or a speaker: Now what? In this section I'm going to teach you how to identify the people you want in your network and give you some tips on how to make the right impression on them.

In the fall of 2011, I spoke at the Business Innovation Factory conference with a friend I'd met through Twitter. We had the chance to speak alongside some pretty big-name authors—one of whom was Dan Pink, the *New York Times* bestselling author of *Drive, A Whole New Mind*, and *Free Agent Nation*. I'd been a big fan of Dan's work for some time, and I really wanted the chance to talk with him about the future of education. I made it one of my main goals for the conference to meet him and make a good impression.

But how do you go about meeting and making a good impression on a famous person who has no idea who you are? In reality, these seemingly chance meetings rarely occur by chance. To network effectively, you have to be focused and deliberate. In this case, my first networking secret was to obtain a list of guests and speakers from the conference organizers beforehand—usually, all you have to do is ask. Then I sat down with that list and identified ten people that I absolutely wanted to meet. I took notes on their bios and memorized their pictures. Then at the conference I put all my energy into meeting those ten people.

Before the event even began I sent those ten people a short email explaining who I was and why I wanted to meet them at the conference. This is the second secret to networking. By emailing the people you want to meet before you meet them, they already have a little bit of context about who you are (the email address–guessing strategies you learned in Chapter 4 could be very useful here).

The third secret to networking is to have a mutual friend vouch for you and introduce you to the person you want to meet. In this case, I had my friend Dennis Littkey introduce me to Dan. When I actually talked to Dan, he recalled that I was working on UnCollege and had a little bit of context for our conversation. Mutual friends like Dennis are invaluable; they're members of your community who can open up doors you never thought were available before. (We'll get into the specifics of how to bring people into your community later in the chapter.)

Let's get one thing clear: You shouldn't view networking as a game. You don't want to meet people to increase your number of friends on Facebook; you want to meet people because they are genuinely interesting and they are interested in your work. If you try to meet people because they are famous, I guarantee it won't work. In my case, I didn't want to meet Dan because he was a bestselling author; I wanted to meet him because he was a fellow education activist (Dan sits on the board of Dennis's nonprofit), and I wanted his perspective on the value of college. Above all, the best way to meet interesting people is to be interesting yourself.

My friend Francis Pedraza, the CEO of Evr.st,* was with me at this conference, and he also had a list of people he wanted to meet. At the top of his list was Whitney Johnson, who runs Clayton Christensen's hedge fund and reviews papers with Carlos Slim. While these aren't household names, they are influential ones. Clay coined the term *disruptive innovation* and has written a book about the subject that is used in college classrooms around the world. He's probably the world's most famous business professor. Carlos Slim is the richest man in the world, much of his fortune amassed from the telecom industry.

Francis was interested in meeting these people because, at the time, he was looking for people to invest in his startup. Like me, Francis had also emailed Whitney before the conference with background on his company. Today, Whitney is an adviser to Francis's company, and another person Francis met at the conference, Alex Osterwolder, is an investor.

As I was sitting with Francis at the airport, waiting for my flight

---

* Full disclosure: I am an adviser to and hold a very small amount of equity in his company.

home, neither of us could recall how we learned to email people we wanted to meet before events, but it has served us well. Francis began recounting the story of how he met David Kelly, one of his friends and advisers. In May 2010 Francis hacked his way into the X PRIZE benefit dinner in Los Angeles through a connection at the X PRIZE Foundation. Someone should really give Francis a PhD in conference hacking: Not only did he get in but he managed to obtain the guest list from the organizers of a private event. How did he obtain the guest list, you wonder? He simply emailed the organizer and asked nicely.

He went through the list and identified the top twenty people to meet. He made flash cards with their bios and pictures and learned them all by heart. This is why it is vitally important to get a guest list; without one you'll have no idea who to connect with. Francis memorized the identities of those twenty people and had a very clear goal of whom to meet with. David Kelly was one of those people. David is a professor at Stanford, and more famously cofounded IDEO, the design consultancy. A year later, David is one of Francis's closest friends and a mentor.

The reason both Francis and I were able to connect with these people is that we've developed personal pitches. Remember, the people you want to meet have a lot to do, and there are undoubtedly many other people like you vying for their attention. If you make the opportunity to talk to them, you better be prepared with a clear and succinct reason for why they should listen to you.

Create Your Two-Minute Pitch

My two-minute pitch goes like this:

> I'm Dale Stephens and I founded UnCollege.org. I recently wrote
> my first book, *Hacking Your Education*, which Penguin is pub-
> lishing in 2013. The book tells the story of how I left school
> when I was twelve and provides a manual for how to go about
> educating yourself outside school. I'm also a Thiel Fellow, part
> of the 20-Under-20 program run by Peter Thiel, the first outside
> investor in Facebook.

This sounds impressive now, but before I got the Thiel Fellowship and a book deal, this technique still worked:

> I'm Dale Stephens and I founded UnCollege.org. I left school
> when I was twelve, skipped middle school and high school, and
> became an expert in self-directed education. I did things like
> work at startups, live in France for six months, and start a
> photography business all before I was eighteen. Now I'm encour-
> aging more people to become self-directed learners.

These short sentences both establish credibility and provide a
basis for conversation. This should be the goal of your two-minute
pitch. As you develop your pitch, make sure it answers these questions:

1. What is your name? This should be pretty obvious.
2. What are you working on? This could be a company, project, or
   field of study.

3. What (or with whom) are you affiliated? This could be a company, a project, or a university.

Work to develop a two-minute pitch so that when someone asks, *Who are you?* Or, *What do you do?* you can answer swiftly and confidently.

|||||||||||||||||||||||||||||||||||||||||||||||||||||||||||||||||||||||||||||||||||||||||||||||||||||||||||||||||||||

Sometimes it doesn't make sense to try to connect with the most famous people in the room. When you recognize someone as a celebrity, you put them on a pedestal, which means that you will never be their equal. That power differential inhibits your ability to break into an already famous person's inner circle. You will probably never be Oprah's best friend. I'm sorry.

One solution to this problem is to never watch television. A better solution is to make friends with the people who aren't yet successful but will be. The challenge in this case is not networking, it's identifying talent. It's figuring out who you should spend time getting to know today because they'll be leading the world tomorrow.

So ask yourself right now, who do you know who will change the world? As your network grows, you'll start to find that most of the people you want to know are within one or two connections. But what about people you don't know yet whom you want to know? One weakness of networks is that they're generally not good at identifying young talent; talented young people often have no network at all. They're people you won't generally find unless you're looking for them. This is precisely why many successful individuals are happy to share their knowledge through mentorship—they want access to young talent.

Identifying Talent

Figuring out who is influential is hard, but it's a skill that you will hone over the years. Here are a few ways you can spot young talent:

- Ask, What are you passionate about?

   People who will change the world generally have a clear answer to this question. A sample of answers among people on my list of world changers includes facilitate the peaceful coexistence of humans and animals, alleviate the crushing effects of world poverty, uplift human potential, reveal the causes of human emotion, and make entrepreneurial skills life skills.

- Listen to articulation.

   People who change the world speak clearly and cleanly. They don't use filler words such as um, so, or like, and they pay attention to grammar. They are able to clearly articulate their talents.

- Watch body language.

   Do they stand confidently? It's quite easy to tell how confident someone is by how she stands. If she is slouching with her hands in her pockets, you should probably move on. However, if she is standing tall, with the crown of her head held high and arms open, then you should pay attention. If you're someone who doesn't have good posture and isn't taken seriously, remember that standing up straight is a really easy way to improve how influential people think you are.

Not only are these fabulous ways to identify young talent but they are three areas that you should use to evaluate yourself. What is your passion? Can you explain your ideas clearly? Do you stand confidently? Once you've identified the people in your life who are going to change the world, make a concerted effort to stay in touch with them. Offer your help and expertise where you can. Offer to introduce them to other talented and interesting people who could be helpful to them. Email them interesting articles and things you read. Your investment in these relationships will pay dividends down the line.

||||||||||||||||||||||||||||||||||||||||||||||||||||||||||||||||||||||||||||||||||||||||||||||||||||||||||

THE IMPORTANCE OF REPUTATION

Building a network of people who can vouch for you is particularly important when you don't have a college degree. You see, a college degree is a signal. It signals that you can complete a four-year-degree program and have a minimum level of competency. But without a degree, people don't know that about you.

In evolution there are all types of signals—of status, sexual prowess, health, you name it. The classic example is the peacock's tail. The peacock's tail signals a peahen that he's an eligible mate. When you don't have a college degree, however, you can't rely on conventional signals to demonstrate your value. You don't have the fancy degree that many people immediately look for. But there are countersignals too. Countersignaling is a way to communicate your value and talent without relying on conventional signals. Take Silicon Valley, for example, where it's sometimes difficult to tell a young millionaire entrepreneur from a homeless person.

As a hackademic, you demonstrate your competency in other ways. When someone meets you, they don't look for your Harvard degree. What do they do instead? They check on Facebook and LinkedIn to see what friends you have in common, and they ask those friends what they think of you. They ask if you're competent. They ask if you're smart. They ask if you can follow through.

Dan Gould, an independently wealthy entrepreneur who dropped out of high school and later out of Brown, told me that he gets more than a dozen back-channel calls to vouch for someone in his network every week. The need for formal credentials may well be diminishing exactly because it is now easier than ever to do a background check on every new person you meet.

Dan has never gotten a job through traditional means. He has started, built, and sold companies. He has worked at multinational corporations like Fox. But Dan has never sent in a résumé.

When I ask him how that can be, he points to his mentors—people like Andy van Dam, a renowned professor of computer science at Brown University. The guidance they've provided Dan is irreplaceable, but their ability to tell others that he actually knows what he's talking about is even more important.

Recommendations on LinkedIn have started to serve this purpose, but the veracity of those recommendations is difficult to assess. You simply cannot replace the networks of trust you create in the real world by introducing your friends with meaningless words on the Internet.

Introduce Your Friends

Some of your friends probably have similar interests but don't know it yet. If so, they should get to know each other. It's your responsibility to make those connections that build relationships. These are the relationships that make the world go round.

1. Identify five pairs of your friends that should get to know each other. This could be because they share a common interest, speak the same foreign language, have a common experience, work in the same field, or are looking to learn from someone in a certain subject area.

2. Write both of your friends an email suggesting they meet. Here's an example of an email I recently wrote:

Benjamin <> Nick

Benjamin, meet Nick. He founded StartupLi.st and just moved to San Francisco from the Midwest.
Nick, meet Benjamin. He works at Livefyre and moved to San Francisco two years ago from Kansas.
I think you two would have a fun conversation about the transition from the Midwest to California.

Best, Dale

3. Send five emails introducing ten friends. The world will thank you. On an average day, I make ten to fifteen introductions.

||||||||||||||||||||||||||||||||||||||||||||||||||||||||||||||||||||||||||||||||||||||||||||||||||||||||

THE TRUE VALUE OF YOUR NETWORK: GETTING JOBS

One of the most common questions I get is, Without a college degree, how am I supposed to get a job? All the job applications I see require a college degree.

See, that's just the thing: When you don't have a college degree, you don't apply for jobs. You're referred for jobs through your network. According to the owner of the human resource firm Epic Development, over 80 percent of jobs are never advertised.[1] They are part of the unadvertised job market.

Instead of making postings on job boards, companies often ask their employees if they have anyone to recommend for open positions. This is how Adam Jackson (the guy who went from Arby's to Apple to TomTom) got his first job at Apple, and it's also how Nick Bilton, now the lead technology reporter for the *New York Times*, got his first job at Mirimax. People inside the company knew who they were, liked what they'd seen, and recommended them for the position.

In fact, Nick has never applied for a job. Every job he's ever had has come from personal connections. "You can get jobs from a regular job search," he told me, "but they are increasingly more difficult to come by—the way we're all connected now, with social media and LinkedIn and everything else. I wouldn't have gotten my first job at Miramax if it wasn't for the person who ran the design department. I wouldn't have gotten my second job designing toy packaging if it wasn't for a professor I'd met. I wouldn't have gotten the roles I had in startups if it weren't for various people I'd met along the way. I wouldn't have ended up as a designer at the *New York Times* if it weren't for someone I met at the rock climbing gym I used to go to." Once at the *Times*, Nick worked hard to get his coworkers and supervisors to believe in him. He started out as a graphic designer, laying out pages. Next he started writing bylines for photos. One day he asked if he could write a sample column. He did, and the editor liked it. Nick began writing more frequently and now he's a full-time columnist.

Nick used the network he developed during internships to find jobs in college. "I would have different internships on different days of the week," he told me. "I didn't learn anything from most of those internships; I was ordering pizza and getting coffee, or helping people cut circles with X-Acto knives." But Nick created relationships with people, so when he needed recommendations for jobs, he had them, and he got connections to the jobs that he wanted. In today's age, everything is connected and visible. If you want a job somewhere, don't just fill out a résumé and send it in—you look up the people you will be working under. Get their names, look them up on LinkedIn, Facebook, and Twitter, and see who you know in common. You have as many people as you can recommend you to whoever is hiring until you get your foot in the door. Relying on sending in a résumé to get a job is not enough.

$100 for LinkedIn

All of Nick's jobs came through personal connections. One of the easiest ways to keep track of those personal connections now that the days of Rolodexes have passed is by using LinkedIn, the professional social network with more than 100 million users.

1. If you don't already have a LinkedIn profile, create one, or if you do, update it. LinkedIn is often the first place people go to check if you have a professional presence on the Internet.
2. Give a friend $100, and have him pay you back $1 for every connection you add on LinkedIn. This shouldn't be difficult. To start, go through your contacts and see who you already know.
3. If you still need to add more connections, go to a party and exchange contact information with the guests. Use their email addresses to look them up on LinkedIn. Add the faculty and staff members at your college

Continue doing this until you've earned the full $100 back from your friend!

COMMUNITY VERSUS NETWORK

Your community is a subset of your network. Your community is made up of the people with whom you've shared your values, your hopes, your dreams, and your fears. Your network, on the other hand, consists of those people whom you've met once or twice in passing. The first part of this chapter addressed how to expand your network through contacts you make at conferences and through resources like LinkedIn. Now, we're going to talk about how you can bring some of those people into your community by hosting parties, salons, and introducing your friends.

Deliberately building your network is a critical first step to creating a community. You've already learned how to ask people out for coffee—that's a great start, but now I'm going to share some other strategies you can use when meeting people for the first time. As I learned to network—having coffee with people, going to conferences, and hosting parties—I developed strategies to increase the likelihood that a single encounter with someone will lead to a lasting friendship.

I didn't start building a community intentionally; as an extrovert, I came by it naturally. I'd organize dinner parties, invite people over, and in the process become responsible for the cross-pollination. Throwing people together and seeing the sparks that fly provides infinite joy for me. At my dinner parties, it's not uncommon to hear things like:

"Oh, you're working on neuroscience? You should meet my friend Sandra!"

"Oh, you're going to Toronto? You should meet my friend Aron!"

"Oh, you're from Siberia? You should meet my friend Kristina!"

Some friends even fondly call my home "the Catalyst." One side benefit of constantly introducing your friends is that you build an ever-growing network of trust around you. People begin to think of you with positive regard. If someone asks Sandra, Aron, or Kristina if they know Dale, they would all respond with an enthusiastic yes.

If you aren't naturally extroverted it's probably best not to start throwing yourself into huge networking events. It's better to start with one-on-one interaction—say having coffee with people—or at small, intimate dinner parties with three to four guests. I'll cover more on these topics shortly.

If the pressure of having to come up with topics of conversation is scary, make a list of things to talk about and questions that can start conversations. Some examples are:

1. What are you passionate about?
2. With is your favorite book (or movie or something else) and why?
3. How did you get into your current field?

Of course, you should also have your own answers to these questions down so that if someone asks the same of you, you'll know exactly what you want to say.

BRING PEOPLE TOGETHER

To make effective introductions for your friends, you must continually expand your community and network to include new people. I do this by hosting dinner parties and inviting my friends to bring new friends with them. Sometimes I host large parties with seventy-five to a hundred people, where all my friends mix and match. Other times I'm a guest. When I'm invited to a party, I always ask if I can invite friends. I often bring friends with me, and in doing so continue to introduce my friends to new people.

While organizing dinner parties, salons, and events is only a hobby for me, for some people like Joey Rubin, it's a full-time job.

Joey, today a creative director for Social People, an advertising agency in L.A., owner of a restaurant chain, and professional event producer, didn't bother finishing high school or even going to college.

After leaving high school, he moved to New York after he applied for, and was given, an internship at a record label and nightclub called NuBlu, a small venue that held about two hundred people. After interning there for six months he was offered a job as the events director at a nearby nightclub. He spent two years in that position but was soon getting so many requests to organize events that he decided to launch his own event production company, TASTE.

He made the jump from intern to respected event producer because he was great at his job and built a network around him as he went. When he met people at his parties who could become potential clients, he introduced himself and thanked them for coming. Some of these people became friends, and they were the first to hire Joey when he decided to strike out on his own.

From the music business, Joey branched out into the more general events space. At one point, he was producing more than two hundred events per year. "I did nightlife to concerts to corporate events. I once shut down Old Vegas. I did an event for twenty-six thousand in Prospect Park on the final day of the World Cup in 2010. I've done private parties for Louis Vuitton. I was a one-man army. I was meeting thousands of people. I met tons and tons of creative people from all different fields," Joey told me.

And Joey didn't just meet those people. He welcomed them into his community, and they became part of his network. Although Joey is only twenty-five, he's figured out the importance of curating a community around you.

Joey is an example of someone who organizes events in the real world, but you can organize events on your college campus just as well. Even during the seven short months I spent at Hendrix College I organized events—everything from a TEDx conference to dinner parties. I did this for exactly the same reason I organize events now: to meet new people, exchange ideas, and expand my community.

Eric Jorgenson, an almost-college dropout and now employee at Zaarly in San Francisco, organized everything from hackathons to weekly salons for precisely the same reason. Eric really shouldn't have a college degree with how little time he actually spent at college. During the two years he spent on the Michigan State University campus, he did everything he could to avoid going to class. But rather than playing video games all the time, Eric organized two Startup Weekends—an amazing exercise in sales, marketing, partnerships, and logistics. For those who aren't familiar, Startup Weekend is a nonprofit organization that sponsors weekend-long events at which real people come together to build real companies. In fifty-four hours, participants launch a company, get real customers, and pitch to investors. Some of the companies built in fifty-four hours have become real companies.* The company that Eric currently works for, Zaarly, was born out of a Startup Weekend. Eric got the job at Zaarly because he met the CEO when he was organizing the Startup Weekend events.

But two Startup Weekends weren't enough. Eric wanted a space to hold events all the time. So Eric set about launching the Hatch, a student incubator and coworking space. To do so, he had to raise $100,000.

"When I started it seemed so daunting to sell something entrepreneurial to the old institution of Michigan State University," Eric told me. "I had to sit down with a lot of people, all the way up to the president, to sell my vision of the space." To gain the approval of the university, Eric found dozens of examples of students who needed a space to work on projects and build companies.

In the end, MSU approved the Hatch, but Eric still had to find independent funding for it. Eric began by identifying alumni who had become independently wealthy as entrepreneurs. He went to the office of alumni affairs and asked for a list of alumni who donate to the university and a list of alumni who are entrepreneurs. He figured these types of donors would be the most interested in helping students work on independent projects and start companies.

"Eventually I identified two individuals," Eric said, "and once they heard the stories of one student who was spending twelve hours per day coding in a coffee shop and another who literally was melting plastic on a hot plate in his dorm room to make molds of prototypes, they wrote two fifty-thousand-dollar checks."

---

* If you want to organize or participate in a Startup Weekend, visit www.startupweekend.org.

Eric and his comrades set up the Hatch in a space across from the university. Finally he had a space where he could hold events on a regular basis. Like me, Eric looked to the Enlightenment period and its salons as an inspiration. Salons, often the center of intellectual, political, and cultural life in the seventeenth and eighteenth centuries, were where smart and talented people would gather to have dinner, mingle, and discuss the issues of the day. In Paris, some women were renowned for their salons; they basically made socializing their profession. In doing so, they became notable in their own right because they facilitated conversation for the leading thinkers and artists of their day.

The point of a salon is to bring people together, to ask them to support and challenge you on your quest to change the world. In the process, ideas are exchanged, friendships are formed, and bubbles are burst. When I first moved back to San Francisco after leaving college I started hosting weekly salons, usually centered around a topic—love, intention, or meaning, for example. I'd invite five to ten people to my home for a potluck, and the discussion would begin.

This is a practice I continue today, though my travel schedule makes it more difficult now so sometimes my salons aren't held every week. To make up for some of that loss I now avoid eating dinner without two or more friends present. In this way I host lots of mini salons and get to have deep and meaningful conversations with many friends on a regular basis.

Start a Salon

1. Choose a day of the week when you are consistently home and can host a salon. A salon is a dinner party with a purpose: the purpose being to share and challenge ideas.

2. Create a Facebook event, and invite three to eight friends over for dinner. Make it potluck, and ask them to bring something. The format is similar to a collaborative learning group, but the aim is different.

3. If you don't want to invite friends over to your home, choose a cheap and quiet restaurant where you can have a lively discussion.

4. Communicate to your friends that this isn't a party, but a salon. Explain that the purpose of the evening will be to find ways to support and challenge one another.

5. To start, pose a question to the group, such as, What is the purpose of education? Write this question on the invitation and make it clear you will discuss this at the salon.

6. After the salon, encourage people to host their own salons. Invite your guests back the following week for another mind meld and brain party.

|||||||||||||||||||||||||||||||||||||||||||||||||||||||||||||||||||||||||||||||||||||||||||||||||||||||||

CHAPTER SIX

Finding Educational Resources

Personally I'm always ready to learn, although I do not always like being taught.

—WINSTON CHURCHILL

DRIP. DRIP. DRIP. DRIP DRIP DRIP DRIP DRIP.

That is the sound of water slowly leaking through the roof of my local library, cascading off the tarps covering the stacks, and hitting the floor. Until 2009, the library in my hometown was housed in a temporary cinder block building from the 1950s. And yes, the roof leaked. Water and books do not mix well.

I first fell in love with the library when I was five or six, and my mom started a story time program. I was instantly hooked: I could have as many books as I possibly wanted for free! As I got older, I started volunteering with the Friends of the Library because I saw the library as an incredibly valuable resource, both for myself and members of the community.

Our long-term goal was always to raise enough money to build a new library, but for a small organization in a town of five thousand people, raising $5 million seemed impossible. We tried passing a ballot measure, but most people just didn't want to pay more taxes. Our capital campaign also fell short. After nearly ten years of work, we finally convinced the county and city to commit funds to build a new library. The new library opened when I was seventeen, the year before I went to college.

Growing up, I found the library to be one of the best learning resources available. Books, fiction and nonfiction, were available for me to read. If I couldn't find a book locally, I could place an interlibrary loan and conceivably find any book I could possibly want within the entire state of California.

The great part about the library is that no one needed to give me permission to use it. No one had to tell me where to look; I could find that out on my own between the Dewey decimal system and the computer catalog. The library really is an autodidact's wet dream.

The library helped me create a personal learning plan for whatever I wanted to learn. It was the first step to finding resources that would help me learn a particular skill. Having a plan kept me accountable and focused.

The top of your personal learning plan should be labeled with the skill you want to learn—French, for example.

Right below the word *French*, I would write why I wanted to learn it:

I want to learn French so that I can live in France.

Setting a deadline and time commitment to learn are necessary. Otherwise it's easy to put things off. For example:

I will spend three hours three days per week learning French.

If you don't use a calendar, now is a great time to start. Google Calendar allows you to set notification so you don't miss the times you've scheduled to learn.

Once the timing was decided, I set about gathering resources. Here are some of the places I'd look for resources:

- Google (for example, search "French 101 Syllabus" to find sample syllabi from real French courses)

- Wikipedia

- YouTube

- The highest-rated books on Amazon

- Local community colleges

- Reddit subgroups based on interest

- Asking friends who speak French how and where they learned it

- Opportunities to travel to France (for example, exchange programs)

HACKING LIBRARIES

You can follow this same process for anything you want to learn, be it statistics or the music industry.

Geno Sims manages relationships with emerging musical artists like A$AP Rocky. He originally wanted to go to college, but then one of his best friends was shot and killed at Virginia State University. Geno is from Harlem, and growing up, he told me he lost nearly 90 percent of his friends to the streets.

"Wow, you go away to school to almost get killed getting an education?" Geno recalled, "I was like, 'This ain't for me.'"

Instead of going to college, Geno turned to the resources he had around him to learn about the music industry. One of those was the New York Public Library.

Geno told me, "I think one thing that people don't do, they don't utilize things that are free, for instance, they don't utilize the New York Public Library, or the library period. The library is the most resourceful, best place ever. You can walk in there and get whatever you want. You can access a computer, you can borrow a book, you can get any book you want, you can look at images, you can scan images. That's the greatest weapon ever, I think, the library."

Geno has another reason that the library is the best. "There's hot chicks in there!" he exclaimed. "Every time I go to the library, there's always hot chicks in there. That's what lured me in there. My boys were doing shit in the streets, and in the street running around, hustling or whatever, and I would always take two hours a day to go to the library—to meet girls and take out a book."

When Geno was kicked out of high school, his teacher told him he'd be nothing more than a car washer. He found that motivating. So instead of going to college, he started by reading books about music at the library. Then he started checking out tapes from the library so that he could listen to music. But he wasn't satisfied just reading about or listening to music; he wanted to engage with the music industry. Using the knowledge about music he'd learned at the library, he got a job as a salesclerk in a record store. It was nothing glamorous, but it allowed Geno to learn about the industry. The store he worked at sold tickets to and hosted events about the music industry to which producers or directors would come and give talks. Geno always attended those types of events because many popular artists and record executives were often present.

Geno's self-education paid off. He learned the ropes of music from people in the industry. He built a network around him from attending the events, and eventually became an artists and repertoire executive helping scout talent and develop artists. Right now, Geno manages new artists for Sony BMG. He loves it.

The ability to use free resources like the library demonstrates that knowledge is power. Knowledge gives you access to people and opportunities. Everyone says that it's not *what* you know, it's *who* you know. But I'm not convinced that's the case. Because what you know will get you in touch with who you need to know.

Use the Library

There are many free resources at our disposal that we neglect to use. Universities may not be free, but libraries are!

1. Are you a member of your local library? If not, join. Anyone can get a library card.

2. Visit the library and check out a nonfiction book about a career that you're considering this week. Read the book and bring it back next week to get another. If you're feeling extra brave, talk to a cute guy or girl about the book you just read.

3. After using the library, sit down and write for five minutes about what you learned from your reading and how what you read impacted your goals. Did it make them sharper? Clearer? Are you still interested in that career or do you want to try something else?

||||||||||||||||||||||||||||||||||||||||||||||||||||||||||||||||||||||||||||||||||||||||||||||||||||||||||||||||||||||

HACKING TRADITIONAL COLLEGES

Libraries aren't the only free learning resources that exist. Even if you're not enrolled, schools themselves can be used as free learning resources.

When I was fifteen, I decided that I really, really wanted to learn French. I ended up hosting a French exchange student and living abroad in France, but to start I thought it would be easier to take a French class.

I'd tried studying French on my own, but it was really difficult to try to learn a new language without anyone to talk with. I could study grammar, but I wanted to be able to truly speak French.

So I started poking around to see where I could find communities of people learning French. First I asked the local high school if I could come to their French class, but I come from such a small town that it turned out my hometown high school offered only Spanish. I had to widen my scope. A few local community colleges offered French classes, so I decided to sign up for the one closest to my home. Except that I sort of forgot I was fifteen and didn't have a high school diploma. Community colleges generally have high acceptance rates, but without a high school diploma, you're out of luck. I was too young to take the GED, so that wasn't an option. I was stumped about what to do.

Then I came across a novel idea: I could email the professor and ask if I she would let me come to class even though I couldn't technically be enrolled. I figured she wouldn't care because I would barely be burdening her with any extra work. She wrote back the next day exclaiming that of course I was welcome to come to class and that she hoped I would participate fully as a member of the class.

I went, I participated, and when I could technically enroll as a student I did, but for a few semesters I was an impostor. No one ever noticed. Not once did someone ask to see my student ID. I just walked in the building every Thursday evening, went to the classroom, and learned.

Sometime during the media storm that UnCollege created, a reporter asked me, "What do you recommend someone do if they don't want to learn completely on their own and still want to be part of a college community?"

The question stumped me for a moment, but then I thought back to my French class. I thought, why couldn't you rent a room in Cambridge, live with a bunch of college students, attend classes that interested you, join student groups, and live the life of a student without paying $50,000 in Harvard tuition and fees? Sure, you wouldn't get a degree after four years, but you also wouldn't be out almost two hundred grand. It would take some work, planning, and financial backing to cover your living expenses, but it would be an excellent learning experience.

I posted a status update on Facebook to this effect, and I learned that an acquaintance of mine named Kirill Zdronyy had done just that at Stanford. When I had coffee with Kirill, he told me he will donate to Stanford one day when he has money, but not because he was ever a student there. In fact, Kirill was quite the opposite of a student: For six months he used the resources of Stanford—joined clubs, went to parties, attended classes, and talked to professors—all without paying a dime.

Kirill's parents came to Canada from Ukraine when he was eight. He went through public school and then to a university but become disillusioned with college after the first semester and was kicked out because he stopped going to classes. He spent six months at a local community college to get his grades back up so that he could reenter the university, but he dropped out because he didn't like his courses. After that, he started a company servicing computers, and one of his clients offered him a full-time job, which he took.

Kirill knew he wanted to be in Silicon Valley, so he told his boss he was going to spend a month there. He rented a room on AirBnB and spent the month "stumbling into people's offices," as he described it. Kirill emailed people all over Silicon Valley, told them he was a student from Canada thinking about relocating, and asked to meet with them to get their advice. One of those people was George Zachary, one of the first angel investors in Twitter (angel investors make very early investments in companies, typically between $50,000 and $100,000, in exchange for equity).

Meeting George Zachary was a complete accident for Kirill. He was supposed to be meeting someone else but was given the wrong address. He showed up for the meeting, and the secretary, instead of telling him to sit down, invited Kirill into the kitchen where she was having pizza for lunch. Kirill was eating pizza in a nice office on Sand Hill Road, the area of Palo Alto that houses investor offices, and George walked in and said something like, "Why are you eating pizza in my office?" Kirill gave George a great two-minute pitch about moving from Vancouver to Stanford, and George and Kirill hit it off. They ended up talking for over two hours, and George told Kirill that he should do whatever it took to move to Silicon Valley permanently.

Kirill took that advice to heart. He went home to Vancouver and decided to save up $10,000 in six months. To do this, he moved back in with his parents and began his computer servicing business again. He hustled to find new clients and put every penny he earned into savings. In December 2010, Kirill packed a bag and moved to Stanford. Before he moved to Stanford, he used CouchSurfing (www.couchsurfing.org) to contact students at Stanford to see if he could crash on a couch for two weeks. Fifteen students replied saying he could stay for two weeks and five students said Kirill could stay as long as he wanted. He ended up on a grad student's couch, rent free, for five months.

Kirill made the most of his five months at Stanford. He basically operated as a Stanford student. He went to classes and met with professors during their office hours. He joined Stanford clubs. He hung out in the student union. But the biggest success that came from spending five months at Stanford was that Kirill's company, Nutrivise.com, became a reality.

While at Stanford, Kirill found a partner to work with him on Hungry Tribe, a product that helps individuals and enterprises analyze the healthfulness of their food. They applied and were accepted to the StartX Incubator, which provides funding and office space for a select few companies. It's a highly competitive incubator—of the hundreds that apply, only a few make it through each round.

After completing StartX, Kirill was able to raise $120,000 in funding for his company from angel investors he met during his time at Stanford. Due to the relationships he developed at Stanford, Kirill signed Stanford's dining services as Nutrivise's first client. His Stanford connections also helped him get an invitation to demo Nutrivise at the prestigious FutureMed conference.

Now, at age twenty-four, Kirill is a successful guy who loves his job. Most people can't say that when they're forty. He got to this point because he figured out that you don't have to be in college to be in college. When I followed up with Kirill a few months later, he was close to closing a deal with Google Dining and other high-profile clients.

Kirill figured out that anybody can talk to professors, arguably a university's most valuable resource. When you want someone's expertise you can just go to her office and knock on the door. No one will ask you to show an ID card. You can show up for classes and sit in on lectures. You can join student groups and make friends. There is absolutely nothing stopping you from using the resources of a university without being enrolled as a student.

Crash a Class

This hack is pretty easy: I want you to do what I did at community college and what Kirill did at Stanford. I want you to go to a university that you don't attend and show up for a class. It doesn't matter which university, and it doesn't matter which class. I can't guarantee what you're going to learn, but I can guarantee that you're going to learn more by crashing a class than you would sitting at home on Facebook.

1. Identify a university near you. CollegeBoard (www.collegeboard .com) is helpful for this.
2. Go onto the university's website and look up the course schedule. Choose a class that interests you and note the time. You can find the course catalogs on the university website that will list the time and location of classes.
3. Be sure to choose classes that are in big lecture halls so no one will notice or care that you drop in.
4. Show up to the next class. Participate in class. Act like a student. Ask a fellow student what last week's homework assignment was.
5. If you enjoyed the class, go again. If not, choose a different class and repeat until you find a class you enjoy.

INCUBATE YOUR IDEAS

When I say *incubator*, I'm not suggesting that you raise chickens. I'm talking about a different type of incubator. An incubator that functions as a human accelerator. The most famous of these is Y Combinator. YC, as they call it in Silicon Valley, offers an accelerator program for startups. In exchange for about 6 percent of your company, they give you $5,000 per cofounder to support yourselves for three months. That may not seem like much, but the best part is, during those three months, YC organizes weekly dinners with mentors and gives you access to their network.

YC has become the Harvard of accelerators. Its companies are so good that Yuri Milner, a Russian investor, offers every YC graduate $150,000 in convertible debt, no questions asked. That's basically $150,000 in free money that can be paid back at any point in the future. The environment that incubators provide, whether YC or not, mimics that of college:

UNIVERSITY	INCUBATOR
Dorms	Coworking space
Cafeteria	Weekly dinners
Professors	Mentors

Perhaps that's why incubators have become so popular among young people.

Incubators provide an alternative to college with no risk. If it goes well, in three months you have a profitable company and are making money instead of shelling it out. If not, you've learned tons in three months and can always go back to school. Or apply to another incubator.

Unlike college, however, these incubators also value ideas that don't work out. YC in particular encourages applicants to apply multiple times, and some people go through YC three or four times before they find an idea that sticks. And there's no shame in this. In fact, YC advertises that they have a preference for teams with a founder that has already done YC. Failing, in the eyes of the incubator and entrepreneur, means more experience. It means you know what *not* to do. More experience means less risk. Less risk means a higher return on investment.

After all, your startup could be the next AirBnB or Dropbox, companies that have become household names from humble beginnings in YC. But I think that incubators aren't really about creating companies at all. They're about learning. An incubator is a form of reverse-tuition university. Essentially they pay you to spend three months trying shit out, failing massively, iterating quickly, and doing it all over again. It's a pretty sweet learning process.

Another way incubators are similar to college is that they provide a common experience. You are going through an intense learning experience with a common group of people. Only instead of being thrown together with eighty other people to learn how to get to class and do your own laundry for the first time, you're being thrown together with other people learning how to start and build a company.

And here's the interesting thing—incubators *aren't just* for tech companies anymore. There are incubators for anyone who wants to start *something*—technology related or not. In Colorado, the Unreasonable Institute will host you for a summer as long as you have an unreasonable idea. In San Francisco's Mission District, La Cocina has an incubator that helps immigrants from foreign countries start food trucks that serve traditional cuisine.

In New York, a few have begun to realize that incubators really are about education and are making no secret of it. At General Assembly, known as GA, you'll find a community space that houses both companies and classrooms. To work at GA, you must apply to be a member of the community. They are creating an exclusive brand just like elite universities. Once you're a member of GA, you're in. The GA brand is well known and well trusted. In addition to single events with topics such as how to raise funding, GA is now offering certificate programs to teach people the fundamentals of design or coding. You pay to take classes on an individual basis for a nominal fee. It's going marvelously well; they just opened their second campus in London and the third in Berlin is opening soon.

Back in California, another brand, Techshop, is growing. With locations in three states, Techshop allows anyone to have access to high-tech tools often found at universities for only $99 a month. Think of Techshop as an education gym. You pay monthly, and while you're a member, you can use the facilities as much as you want. In addition to open lab space with everything from laser cutters to welders, Techshop offers introductory courses to acquaint you with equipment before turning you loose with the tools. Techshop grew out of the Hackerspace movement. Hackerspaces are physical locations that enable people to build, learn, grow, and share. They are funded by members and usually free for anyone to use. You can join, if you choose, for a nominal fee. Today, there are more than 1,237 Hackerspaces in nearly every country around the world. To find one near you, visit www.hackerspaces.org.

Apply for an Incubator

Increasingly, cities are becoming the new universities. With spaces like Y Combinator, Techshop, and General Assembly, hackademics have lots of opportunities to come together and learn. But these aren't the only incubators that exist; there are many others in cities around the world. Here's how to find an incubator space near you:

1. Google "startup incubator in _____" and insert the name of your town or state.
2. Find out when the deadline to apply is, and send in an application. If you don't have an idea now, think of one.
3. Even if you're rejected early in the process, you'll still have learned something through the process of applying.
4. There are incubators for specific types of companies (health companies, for example) and incubators for social enterprises. We keep a list at www.uncollege.org/funding.
5. Some incubators are very competitive; YC accepts only 2 percent of applicants. But that's because YC is in the center of Silicon Valley. If you want a better shot at getting funding for your idea, apply to incubators in less sexy areas: Kansas City or Minneapolis or Calgary.

START A BUSINESS

When you apply to an incubator with a business idea, your goal is likely to be to create a sustainable business. You might view the process of starting a business as a learning exercise, or you might see it as a way to finance other forms of learning. Or it could be both.

When I was young, I started a business to support my educational adventures. I started a flower delivery business when I was twelve, hoping to earn enough money to buy a saxophone. I started a business selling my photography, hoping to earn enough money to support a half-year trip to France. I eventually did both.

I learned tons in the process, not just about music and French but also about running a small business. The best part was that I had finally had the financial means to support myself; I didn't have to ask my parents to pay for trips, lessons, or books.

Ryan Allis dropped out of the University of North Carolina to start iContact (www.icontact.com), an email marketing company providing email newsletter, social media, and design services that he sold in 2012 for $169 million (apparently there's more demand for email marketing than flower delivery). The challenge Ryan poses to college students is this: Start a business. Completing your coursework and homework takes only about 30 hours per week. That leaves another 138 hours to work, eat, and sleep. Eating and sleeping take about 63 hours. That leaves 75 hours for you to work.

What does Ryan recommend doing with those extra 75 hours per week? Start a company, he says, or get a job. "I'm amazed," Ryan told me, "when people who have spent sixteen years in school start looking for jobs three weeks before graduation. That's no way to get a job. Sending out résumés is a terrible way to get a job."

Ryan was an entrepreneur from a young age. Through middle and high school, he ran a web design business. He enrolled at the University of North Carolina in the fall of 2002. Two months later, he met his business partner. After two semesters he dropped out. But he didn't just drop out; he dropped out with a specific goal and a caveat. He gave himself a year to get iContact off the ground. If, by that time, he hadn't grown the business to $10,000 per month in revenue, he decided he would reenroll in school.

Ryan spent a year bootstrapping the business with his cofounder. They lived on ramen noodles and cooked on George Foreman grills to save money. They built an initial product and acquired a few customers—mostly through word-of-mouth referrals—but they weren't making anywhere close to $10,000 per month in revenue.

So Ryan, true to his word, went back. He took classes at 8:00 and 9:00 a.m. to leave the rest of the day clear to work on iContact. A year later, in August 2004, they built the company up to about $60,000 in monthly sales. Ryan decided that was enough over his $10,000 per month goal that he could justify stopping school.

Once Ryan had the means, he began spending time engaging in learning experiences that he simply couldn't at the university. He began traveling to understand different cultures and understand global poverty. He began investing in businesses in emerging markets to give back in a sustainable manner. He started mentoring fellow entrepreneurs.

Entrepreneurship seems to be a popular option for people who choose to hack their education. It's something you can do either while in school or after leaving, and it doesn't require permission from your parents. You can start a business, project, or organization all by yourself.

Dylan Reid is the former CEO of the Kairos Society, the international organization for student entrepreneurs. Although Dylan attends Cornell University, to call him studious would misrepresent how he approaches school. We met in the Bowery District of New York, and although it was a weekday, I got the impression Dylan spends more time there than in class. What then, I wondered, did he learn in college if he has spent the vast majority of time outside the institution? However, by hanging out in the Bowery and meeting people like me, Dylan was contributing real value to the university and community.

According to Dylan, he learned how to take advantage of the resources of the institution. Universities, he says, have two resources: intellectual capital and financial capital. It's fairly easy to tap into the intellectual capital; after all, that's why there are professors at universities. What most students don't know is that universities have a huge amount of financial capital as well.

"People complain all the time," Dylan told me, "that they can't find money to support their projects, or that they can't find a job. That's bullshit. There's money everywhere. You know that. I know that. The trick is figuring out how to get people to give it to you."

Cornell spends over $150 million per year on nonfaculty spending—things like books, lights, benches, and food. Most of that money goes to people totally unrelated to Cornell. One benefit of college is that you can leverage being part of a community. You're in an ecosystem where it is in the school's interest to help you succeed; they want you to be prosperous and successful to enhance the rankings of the school, right? Because there's a great bias with schools, meaning they are more likely to spend money on their own students and alums, Dylan suggested looking to the needs of your school if you're searching for business ideas. Does your school need new benches? Build them. Does your school need a new website? Design it. Does your school need a new coffee shop? Start one.

Make the Most of $100 in a Week

Here's a way to test your entrepreneurial spirit: If I gave you $100, how much could you turn that $100 into in one week? I'm not actually going to give you $100, but that doesn't mean you can't take the challenge.

1. Take $100 out of your bank account. Consider this your seed investment. You can spend this money in any way you choose or not at all. Your goal in one week is to return with the most money possible.
2. Think of ways to earn money. You could have a car wash, do jobs on TaskRabbit.com, or sell water on a hot day at the park.
3. Invite three to four friends to join you in this challenge. A little competition is always healthy.
4. At the end of the week, share what you did, how much you made, and what you learned in the process with your friends.

Seth Godin, a bestselling business author, likes to say that his college experience was "extraordinary, but only because I hacked it." He saw the three thousand students there as an untapped market and eventually built the largest student-run business in the country. Instead of taking required classes that had no relevance for him, Seth designed his own major in computer science and philosophy. He signed up for as many classes as he could, went to them as often (or as little) as he wanted, and spent his free time growing his business. Seth saw the resources of the university and took advantage of them, but he could do that only because he had bigger plans in mind than maintaining his GPA.

Later, Seth applied that same mentality to business school. Some people might think that to start a business you need an MBA. But that's not how Seth saw it. Instead, in 2008, he put up a post on his blog inviting people to apply to spend six months in his office instead of going to business school. What was his motivation? "I wanted to show myself, the world, and my students that you don't need two years to get an MBA and that most everything they teach you in an MBA program is worthless," he said. So Seth created an experiential, challenging program as an alternative to getting an MBA. The cost? Totally free. He was overwhelmed with applications; who wouldn't want to spend six months learning about business from a marketing genius who has written eight bestselling books?

Nine people completed the six-month program. It served as a catapult into the publishing world: One participant is now the head of marketing for Amazon's Domino Project and has launched six bestselling books. Another launched a New York–based creative agency and has attracted high-profile clients. Others took what they learned and applied them to their own jobs.

Seth's alternative MBA program was a one-time experiment, but I do have suggestions for how to create your own alternative MBA program if you want to learn about business without going to business school. As I talked about early in this chapter, going to the library is a great place to start. Check out books like *What Color Is My Parachute?*, *The $100 Startup*, *The Personal MBA*, *The Innovator's Dilemma*, or *Four Steps to the Epiphany*.

If you're more of an aural learner, go on iTunes U and download MBA courses from places like Yale, Stanford, and MIT. All the content of an MBA for zero cost. You can listen while you drive or take the bus.

Investing in a microfinance project using Kiva can help you learn a lot about business as an investor. You have to evaluate a business and determine whether you're making a sound investment. If you want to take this to the next level, travel to the country where you made the investment and meet the entrepreneur. The cost to you for part one is about $50, for part two it's $1,500.

You can also attend seminars and conferences for far less than the cost of an MBA. Every year, Stanford hosts a weeklong celebration of entrepreneurship called Eweek. They even provide scholarships to help young entrepreneurs pay for travel. Google "entrepreneurship conferences" and see what is taking place close to you.

If you want formal advising, hire a mentor or life coach. Look for a veteran in the industry you want to enter and hire him to coach you. Ask for recommendations from friends in the industry you would like to enter. If someone volunteers to mentor you, jump on that. Mentors and coaches have valuable insights that can save you time and money. A great place to start looking for a mentor is www.clarity.fm.

Another option is to engage in a week- or weekend-long executive MBA program, but these programs are often very expensive and do not necessarily offer much return on investment.

HACK OF THE DAY ||||||||||||||||||||||||||||

Learning Budget

The average cost of attending the cheapest, in-state, public university is $17,131. How else you could spend that $17,000? Let's explore some ways:

1. Travel around the world for a year. Alex MacCaw, whom we met earlier, traveled around the world for a year on $22,000, and he was eating out every night. If you pinched a few pennies you could easily travel on $17,000.
2. Buy a new MacBook Pro and have $15,000 left over to start a business. Coincidentally, $15,000 is the amount many incubators give their companies. Apply to an incubator. Read *The $100 Startup*.
3. Hire an expert. At $50 per hour, $17,000 is almost enough to hire someone to teach you something for an hour every day for a year!
4. Create your own learning budget. How would you spend $17,000? You can share your results at UnCollege.org.

|||||||||||||||||||||||||||||||||||||||||||||||||||||||||||||||||||||||||||||||||||||||||||||||||||

CHAPTER SEVEN

Learning from the World

How could youth better learn to live than by at once trying the
experiment of living?
—HENRY DAVID THOREAU

I LOVE FLYING. I LOVE BEING ON AN AIRPLANE, SITTING IN THE SEAT, AND
looking down at the world passing below me. Every time I get on an
airplane I'm left in awe. How is it that in a few hours you can be in
an entirely new country?

That awe first developed when I lived in France for half a year
when I was sixteen. I'd always loved the French language—it just
sounded so lyrical—so I began exploring exchange programs on the
Internet that would allow me to live in France. I eventually found
one that would work with unschoolers, and soon I was bound for
Picardie.

But going to France was expensive, and my parents didn't have
the money to buy me a plane ticket, so they said if I wanted to go I'd
have to figure out a way to make it happen. I checked our AAdvan-
tage accounts but we collectively had only about nine thousand miles,

and I needed sixty thousand for a ticket to Europe. As I was browsing the site, I noticed a credit card offer with a sign-up bonus of forty thousand miles.

I convinced my mom to apply for the credit card, and a few weeks later, I had forty-nine thousand miles. I purchased the remaining eleven thousand miles for about $300 and had myself a plane ticket to France. All in all, I spent $395 on my plane ticket if you include the annual fee for the credit card. A pretty darn good deal.

FROM WAITING TABLES TO NEW YORK CITY

The time that I spent in France was so influential in my life. I learned more about myself and how I interact with the world than in years of unschooling. Spending time abroad gave me a deep appreciation for other cultures and really helped me understand the immense learning opportunities from putting yourself in new and unfamiliar circumstances.

One of the easiest ways to put yourself in a new environment is to physically get in a car or plane or train and go somewhere new. While this may sound expensive, there are ways to make it cheaper, from ride sharing to racking up frequent flyer miles.

Katherine von Jan is an expert at collecting and using airline points. When she was just twenty-two, she led knowledge management for IBM, flying around the world in business class three times per month. Later in her twenties and thirties she worked for top-notch consulting firms, eventually starting her own firm to do work with organizations like the Lumina Foundation. She's now built up enough independent wealth that she can focus on the problems she's passionate about (like education) and people she cares about (like her kids).

The travel that Katherine did has had a transformative impact on her life. Although she eventually ended up getting a college degree, she came home from her first semester of college and told her parents she wasn't going back.

Her parents weren't so pleased, and told her she needed to get a job, so she got a job working the night shift at Dunkin' Donuts. After two weeks of working the counter, she was promoted to donut filler, responsible for creating the donut of the week, such as the bacon double cheeseburger donut. It was a huge seller. The next week they asked if Katherine would like to apply for the manager-training program. But instead she lied and said her grandmother in Hawaii was sick, and she needed to resign to go be with her.

"I cashed my paycheck, bought a one-way ticket to Hawaii, said aloha to my parents, and arrived in Maui with $400 in my pocket," Katherine told me. "I got a job the next day, and in a month had my own apartment, then bought a car and my own health insurance."

Katherine had a friend in Hawaii who said she could stay with her for a few weeks, but other than that she had no safety net. Her first day there she walked into a retail shop in a strip mall. They liked the way Katherine was dressed and offered her a job. About two weeks into that she realized working in retail paid horribly and decided she wanted to work as a waitress so she could collect tips.

Katherine went to another popular strip mall and began asking restaurants if they were hiring. One was hiring a hostess, and Katherine decided to take the job hoping she'd get promoted to waitress soon. One of her coworkers was leaving on a yearlong trip, and Katherine rented her apartment for $500 per month. Another employee there was selling an old car that Katherine and a friend bought for $400. Katherine worked the job for two months until she was promoted to waitress. Making tips, she quit the retail job so she could surf by day and wait tables at night.

This was Katherine's real education: living on her own without contact with her parents. They thought she'd lost her mind but Katherine stayed in Hawaii for a year of healing, discovery, adventure, and insight. About eight months into it she realized she didn't want to wait tables for the rest of her life and applied to college.

Katherine chose the University of New Hampshire because she could get in-state tuition, and UNH was a top-ten program in those days. This time, she took her education into her own hands. She didn't even bother to live in a dorm. She got an apartment. And she made the most of her education, taking MBA-level classes even though she was enrolled in an undergrad program.

She finished her undergrad program and enrolled in a master's program in matrifocal studies. "After a semester my adviser asked me why I would pay a university for a degree in which I have to do all the work," Katherine recalled. "Of course, I had been used to doing this most of my own life, designing my own way of learning. It never occurred to me that I could do this on my own without any institution validating me, or giving me credentials. This was freeing. I withdrew, and decided that the world would be my classroom."

So Katherine sought out a job that would enable her to apply what she had learned and enable her to travel. She went to work for Lotus Development Corp, which was soon after bought by IBM. She could learn about matrifocal leadership in the real world, and she got paid well to do it, instead of paying a university.

The job also enabled her to travel. She got to experience life in different cultures around the world and add a few days onto her business trips so she could explore new countries. Those round-the-world business-class tickets also racked up frequent flyer miles for Katherine. She saved them, and later on when she launched her own business ventures, they came in handy. She used her miles to fly to her first client meeting in Chicago when she didn't have the money to buy a plane ticket.

HACK OF THE DAY ▌▌▌▌▌▌▌▌▌▌▌▌▌▌▌

Collect Points

In January 2005, *The Economist* reported that some fourteen trillion frequent flyer miles had been accumulated worldwide, corresponding to a value of $700 billion.[1] You should have a chunk of that!

1. You have probably, at some point in your life, stayed at a hotel or taken a flight. Find the receipt for that trip, set up an account

with the airline you flew with or hotel you stayed at, and follow the instructions to claim the points.

2. At this point you may only have a few thousand miles, but realize that they add up quickly. Even if you don't fly a lot you can earn miles in other ways. Check out the bonuses for signing up for credit cards; you can often earn thirty to fifty thousand points just for opening an account. Often you don't even have to use the card; you can just cancel it after a year.

3. If you really want to explore this subject, go to FlyerTalk (www .flyertalk.com) and start learning about mileage runs.

4. Before you know it you'll have enough miles for the next trip you need to take whether that's for business or to study abroad.

||||||||||||||||||||||||||||||||||||||||||||||||||||||||||||||||||||||||||||||||||||||||||||||||||||||||||||||

WEEKEND TRIPS TO LONDON

Buying plane tickets was also a formative part of Kim Scheinberg's education. After spending a semester in college and many more semesters traveling, Kim returned to New York and began working on the technology side of media companies, first at magazines like *Esquire* and finally at the *New York Times*.

Kim started her journey into higher education at Boston University. Laughing, she recalled, "I lasted about twelve minutes." Kim left Boston University because she didn't find it interesting. She configured her classes around the most convenient social schedule: She had classes on only Tuesdays and Thursdays. Thursday afternoon she would catch a $19 flight to New York, and at JFK catch a $99

People Express flight to London. Kim would spend the weekend in London and be back in time for her Tuesday morning class.

After Kim left Boston University, she lived in London, previously her weekend getaway. When the money she'd saved from working at a Boston ice-cream shop ran out in London, she bought a plane ticket to Israel and got a job as a waitress in a bar. It wasn't glamorous, but it paid the bills and was a true learning experience. Like Katherine, Kim realized she didn't want to do that for the rest of her life, so she moved back to New York and became involved with the New York Macintosh User Group.

Kim's involvement with that community led to a job offer at the publishing company CMP. After a few years of working and learning, she accepted a job at *Entertainment Weekly*. Later she made the jump up the ladder to *Esquire* magazine and finally the *New York Times*.

When applying to work at the *New York Times*, Kim just said she graduated from Boston University as if she had stayed in school. "The first thing I said when I got into the interview," Kim remembered, "was 'There's something I need to tell you. I lied on my résumé. I don't have a college degree. I did a semester and a half. I knew if I didn't put down I was a college graduate I would never get past human resources. If you want to end the interview right now, I totally understand; I just don't want to waste your time.' [My interviewer] said 'That's totally fine.'" Kim was well qualified; she'd been a Mac user for years and an active member of the Macintosh development community. She got the job.

Kim retired from the *Times* in the early 2000s to pursue impact investing as her primary activity and currently runs a small seed-stage investment fund called Presumed Abundance.

While Kim didn't get a college degree in a four-year time frame, she did take a multiyear educational journey. Just as college has its highs and lows, so does traveling. There are moments of intense excitement and moments of inexorable insecurity.

PARIS OR COLLEGE?

For Julien,* the happiest moments in life are when he lands in a new country. The lowest moments are when he realizes that finding food and shelter will be a challenge. Julien has moved to new countries multiple times for the express purpose of learning. Most recently, he moved to Paris after dropping out of a large public university. During his time at college, all Julien had learned was that he didn't want to be a diplomat; in just a few weeks of living on his own in Paris, he learned how to create a budget, make friends, and adapt to a new environment.

"Why does college cost as much as a house?" Julien asked me on Skype the first time I talked to him. Shortly after our conversation, he left Michigan State University and worked three jobs during the summer to save money to buy himself a one-way plane ticket to Paris to learn French. A few months later, I was in Paris, browsing through

---

* Julien's name has been changed to protect his identity.

old emails, and came across Julien's. I sent him a note asking if he wanted to meet for coffee.

By many standards, Julien is not successful. He lives on just under $1,000 per month, which in Paris, one of the most expensive cities in the world, is damn impressive. But when I asked him if he sees himself as successful, he responded immediately with a resounding yes. Success for Julien is making sure he's living up to his full potential. He likes to know that he's given life his all. Raising the croissant that he's munching on, he says, "Look at this, I'm eating something." Wiggling his feet he says, "I've got comfy shoes." Sounds pretty good to me too.

Like me, Julien assumed college was the next step to success and enrolled in a large state school. But for him, learning to navigate the Kafka-esque bureaucracy of the university was far more difficult than learning how to live in a foreign country. For example, he tested out of the Japanese program at his university and he went to Columbia University to get a fluency certificate. Although Julien was getting job offers from Japanese companies, the university wouldn't give him credit in a major or minor without charging him $3,000 for twenty credit hours. Julien thought that was ridiculous. Thinking about his previous experience, he decided he could learn just as much by going abroad and learning another language in the process. So instead of writing papers about foreign countries and being bullied by the Japanese department, Julien moved to Paris. He moved to Paris because he wanted to learn another language while he was still young and had the facility to do so easily.

The skills you learn from leaving a comfortable environment and moving to a new place are enormous. You learn how to cook, clean, budget, make friends, and stay healthy. Julien has chosen to do this multiple times. When you buy yourself a one-way plane ticket, land somewhere, plop down, and figure out the lay of the land, you get a larger taste of reality. That can suck at times, but what doesn't kill you makes you stronger. It's sometimes hard to appreciate the beauty of something when you're still in the construction process.

FROM DECKHAND TO CAPTAIN

Constructing an education can take many years and multiple continents. It can take a mix of self-education and formal schooling. For Sam Singh, a former oil tanker captain and general manager at Shell Oil, the journey involved all of these.

Sam was born in India. Just before Sam was about to finish high school, his father's small business collapsed, and the family was left without any financial means. Going to college wasn't even an option; Sam had to start supporting himself financially. His choices were the armed forces and the merchant navy. He applied to both. This wasn't one of those choices born out of romance and desire, he didn't grow up thinking he wanted to sail the high seas or fly jets; Sam just did what he had to do. He joined the merchant navy because they paid better than the air force.

"Turns out it wasn't that difficult a job; you had to scrub decks and clean toilets and get yelled at in the beginning, when you're a deckhand, but as you move up, running a ship is basically an exercise in patience and logic," Sam recalled. Sam rose quickly through the ranks and had become captain of a ship by the time he was thirty. "I was the youngest captain of liquefied natural gas tankers in the world," Sam told me. "I was basically working for oil companies, and professionally there wasn't a lot of room to grow once you become captain, because you can't be more than a captain on a ship."

Sam wasn't sure that he wanted to spend the rest of his life on a ship, but without a formal education it would be difficult to switch careers. Often when people come off ships they end up taking clerical jobs, but Sam didn't want to settle for that. He decided he wanted to get an MBA to accelerate his growth, but the first roadblock he hit was that he didn't have a bachelor's degree. Sam approached a few MBA schools in Canada, where he was living at the time, but all denied him entrance.

Sam had just about given up when a friend suggested that he apply to the top MBA programs in the world and take the time to tell his story of self-education. Sam agreed and sent off applications to Wharton, Harvard, and Stanford. This time, he submitted an extra essay detailing his education that had taken place on the ship as he traveled around the world instead of in school. He got into all three MBA programs.

Although he lacked the normal credentials, what Sam possessed in abundance was great experience. He first tried playing the application game by its rules, but that didn't work because the application didn't leave room to communicate the tremendous experience he had working on the ship. But by simply writing about his experience— stating *this is my experience, this is what I learned, and this is why*

I'm qualified—he was able to gain entrance to the most selective MBA programs in the world.

After Sam left Stanford he managed to grab a really senior position at Shell because he was both a captain and an MBA even though he had *no* commercial or business experience at all. Sam spent an amazing four years at Shell as a general manager with a budget of millions, but in September 2011, he left Shell to forge his own path. Now, he's buying a fitness studio in London and a bee farm in Africa, a place he visited while still a ship captain.

After working in an office for four years Sam has the itch to travel again. With his new bee farm, he has an excuse to. Even in his forties, Sam continues to learn from his journeys around the world.

THE TRAVELING ARTIST

Raghava KK surprised his parents when he announced he didn't want to go school. His decision not to go to college was a good one: Today, Raghava is a world-famous artist. His paintings hang in galleries and private collections all over the world and sell for six-figure sums.

"I come from an extremely academic family," Raghava told me. "Every male member is groomed to go to one of the IITs, the most prestigious colleges in India. To question something is important, but creating something is more important. I'm highly dyslexic. I never thought I was not intelligent, I just hated studying. My father is a philosopher, and one day I sat him down when he was having a whiskey. My older brother had run away and broken with traditions. He'd gone to Dartmouth, but going to a liberal arts school was a scandal in my family. I was sixteen. I said, 'Pa, what's the purpose of my education?' In his typical philosophical prose he started blurting out all these nice phrases about learning how to learn, structures, patterns, he listed a bunch of things except independence. I said, OK, I will create a curriculum for myself, I will quit school, and every quarter I will show you what I've learned."

Raghava's dad wasn't very happy with this idea, but Raghava moved ahead with his plan anyway. He bought himself a plane ticket, and there wasn't anything his parents could really do to stop him. He left home and backpacked through Europe and India. He learned sales by convincing Indian embassies to buy him plane tickets in exchange for presentations about what he'd learned on his travels. He learned about hard work when he did manual labor. He learned about cultures from the kind people he met along the way.

"I started realizing I grew up in a bubble," Raghava told me. "I grew up in the hegemony, a well-educated Brahmin family. I didn't know moms could be dads, dads could be moms, grandparents could be moms. It opened my eyes to diversity. I decided to adopt all these realities."

Raghava created a list of things he had never experienced and began to try them out. He worked without money to experience slave labor. He worked on a farm to experience manual labor. Eventually, he began to realize he wanted to pursue a career as an artist.

"I took a trip to meet the world's most famous cartoonists," Raghava told me. "I bombarded Charles Schultz with emails, and I got to meet him. The one thing they all said was that children are creative. They said, work with kids. So I started a cartoon school in India. I got the prime minister of India to inaugurate it. I got the wealthy families to send their kids to me, and I got my servant's children to come. It transcended all barriers. Then schools all over the world started flying me all over the world. I went to Paris and Rome, Mexico City, and Tokyo. I wouldn't accept payment, but I would teach children how to cartoon."

Raghava was barely twenty at this point in his life. He'd traveled widely, but he didn't have a steady source of income to support his travels. His girlfriend who lived in America began soliciting galleries to have showings of Raghava's paintings. The first showing brought in several thousand dollars. The next showing at a larger gallery brought in double or triple that. His art kept moving up the food chain, and a few years later his work was selling for $250,000 per piece. By the time he was twenty-two, he had sold more than a million dollars in art.

What I admire about Raghava is that, although he comes from a traditional family with traditional values, he hasn't let those values define him. "I don't believe in black or white," he told me. "I believe in painting my own shade of gray. That means defining my own values."

Buy a Plane Ticket

You can go just about anywhere in the world for $1,500. That's more than enough money to travel for a week anywhere you want. But let's imagine where you could go for only $500. Here's your challenge:

1. Decide where you want to go. Have you longed to visit Australia or do you want to explore China? Or does Europe sound like more fun? It doesn't matter where you want to go, just decide.

2. Go to Kayak (www.kayak.com/explore), enter your home city, and adjust the slider to have $500 as your maximum budget. The site will display everywhere you can fly to in the world for $500. For $500 from San Francisco I could travel to destinations including Brazil, Alaska, and Toronto.

3. Figure out how you can save $500. Maybe you forego that $5 Starbucks every day and in three months have $500.

4. Go! Buy the plane ticket! Get on that plane! Don't worry about staying at hotels, use CouchSurfing. The cost of your trip can be almost nothing except for your plane ticket and food.

5. Make a list of things you want to learn and accomplish on your trip. These could be things that relate to your destination (for example, if you're going to Brazil maybe you want to learn Portuguese or if you're going to Alaska you might want to learn wilderness survival skills) or they could be things that you've been meaning to get around to but haven't found the time.

Education Hacking Is Lifelong

Every child is an artist. The problem is how to remain an artist once he grows up.

—PABLO PICASSO

EIGHT MONTHS AFTER I FIRST SPOKE WITH JULIEN, THE YOUNG STUDENT who left college and moved to Europe, I found myself in Paris again. The friend with whom I was supposed to be staying wasn't answering her doorbell, so I walked into the corner MacDonald's to snag some free wifi. I logged into Skype to pass the time, and noticed Julien online. He asked if I wanted to sleep on his couch for the night. As it was already 11:00 p.m., I agreed.

I hopped on the metro and met him at La Chappelle station. The night was cold, and Julien was in good spirits, excited to show me the progress he'd made in the eight months he'd spent in Paris. This time he greeted me in French, and we conversed fluently. He could pass for Parisian.

Opening the gate to his apartment, he proudly said, "I have a place to live now, too. It's nothing special, but it's a home." We took the elevator to the fifth floor, and he opened the door to his Paris apartment. It was lovely, and quite spacious by Paris standards, with a full bedroom, bath, kitchen, and living room.

Julien is paying for the apartment with a job selling clothes on the Champs-Élysées and tutoring Japanese businesspeople in French and English. With the language, apartment, and job in place, Paris is starting to feel like home for him.

We stayed up talking until the wee hours of the morning about what we'd each learned in the last year. Julien's accomplishments were clear: He learned French, how to live in a new culture, how to make friends in a new city, and more. But I wasn't so sure exactly what I'd learned. That question made me stop and think.

Because for all that I've done in the last year—write, speak, consult—I'm still of an age where people expect me to be learning. That is not to say that learning stops when I turn twenty-two, the age of most college graduates, but rather to say that I'm young. I don't have as much real-world experience as people who are twice my age simply because I've spent less time on this planet.

And thus I still feel as though I should concentrate on learning. I've tried to make a conscious effort to do this since leaving school by keeping a learning journal as a record of what I learn each day, but my learning doesn't happen in as deliberate a manner as it did when I was unschooling. Before, as an unschooler, I'd sit down and plan a semester's worth of coursework, mimicking traditional schools because often I wanted to use laboratories or talk with professors. It was easier to align schedules that way.

I can't sit down and plan a course in public speaking, because I don't know when I'll be speaking or on what topic. I didn't sit down and plan to learn how to write a book, I just had to do it. Having to learn *while* you do something as opposed to *before* you do something seems to be the biggest difference between the real world and school to me.

And if that seems like a major shift to me, as someone who's used to directing his own education outside a university, I can only imagine how it must feel to people who have been through twelve years of formal school. I've done things in the last year that I had no experience doing. I signed up to go to Russia with no knowledge of the country. I agreed to write a book never having written anything longer than twelve pages.

Doing these things was scary. I didn't know what I was doing saying yes to these absurd things. I figured I would learn how to do it along the way, or accept my inability to learn as a failure. And while many of the projects I agreed to sign up for were a success—like me finishing this book—others weren't. I learned that I didn't have time to build a startup while writing, for example.

I learned immensely from positive experiences in the last year. I learned to write a book. I learned how to speak in front of a thousand people. I learned how to make friends. I learned how to build an intentional community. I learned how to travel to Europe three times in a month.

I've also learned immensely from less-than-positive experiences in the last year. I've learned how to negotiate contracts and how to mediate disputes. I've learned how to tolerate jetlag.

I've seen more progress in the last year than I ever expected. Education technology has become an important sector of the economy, with investors focusing exclusively on this area. At the same time, open education has become mainstream. Stanford's online courses in the fall of 2011 attracted over a hundred thousand students. That success ultimately led some of the professors who taught those courses to leave Stanford to start the companies Udacity and Coursera. The Mozilla Foundation and the U.S. Department of Education have funded the development of the Open Badges project to create a new form of credentialing. Spearheaded by Groupon's Dave Hoover, some industries are bringing back apprenticeships and other positions that don't require degrees.

Progress is happening all around us. At UnCollege.org, we keep a list of all the resources you can use to hack your education. It's ever growing. I'm excited to see what we will be on the list by the time this book is actually published.

But however much progress is made, it's important to recall that the decision of whether to go school, let alone college, very much belongs to the first world. Sam Singh, the degreeless-deckhand-turned-captain-turned-manager at Shell grew up in relative poverty in India and reminded me of this.

"If you had a gun sticking at your head," Sam said, "and there were actually issues about who is going to feed the family, you might look at the decision of going to college a little differently. In the consequence of the Western environment where there's no financial pressures, people go almost—in my opinion—because it's what everyone else is doing and there's nothing else to do. College is a luxury.

The irony is that the majority of the world's population sits on that side of the fence; it's what we miss in Western society. If everyone was put on the spot and actually had to earn a living, very few people would go to college, because they would then view it as an investment in the future that costs a lot of money. It would be hard to justify spending two hundred thousand dollars without a guaranteed return because you don't know the opportunity cost of college."

Sam's reminder is paramount. It's easy to forget the experiences of others and to project our own experience onto the world. And yet, all over the world, people survive without going to college. It's wrong to assume that only the formally educated part of the world "has brains and can do stuff," Sam said, because that ignores a whole bunch of skills that aren't cultivated in school. "If college weren't an option, what would you do?" Sam asked. "How would you earn a living? How would you obtain food? Would your parents support you? Would you get a job?"

These are important questions about individual responsibility as we enter a world of increasing malaise. College debt is rising, and fast. The Occupy Wall Street movement brought to light the fact that college debt now stands at more than a trillion dollars. Student loan debt is more than credit card debt. Scarier still, student loan debt is unforgivable in the case of bankruptcy. The bank can repossess your house but they can't repossess your education. The average student graduates with $27,000 in debt.

There is a bubble in education, and it's on the brink of bursting. The cost of college cannot continue to rise while the value declines.

Since 1980, the cost of college has risen 350 percent while the difference in real wages between high school graduates and college graduates has been decreasing since 2000. In *Academically Adrift*,[1] researchers found that 36 percent of students showed no improvement on the Collegiate Learning Assessment after four years of college. We're paying through the nose for degrees with little to no value.

Sadder still is that of the 75 percent of high school students who enroll in college in the United States, *only half* will finish.[2] Yes, the dropout rate from universities is 50 percent. Five zero. 50. That means that for every college graduate with $25,720 in debt, there's a dropout similarly enslaved to a financial institution without even a degree to show for it. There are lots of people who've given up years of their lives and taken on thousands in debt but aren't any better off than when they started. This book is for those people. For people who worked hard, studied hard, but didn't make it to see the result of their toils. People disempowered by the system.

Only 54 percent of young people between eighteen and twenty-four are currently employed; that's the lowest it has been since the government started keeping score. That's fucking scary. Growing debt, rising unemployment, and the disenfranchisement of youth are the issues of the day, and education is the nexus. It is responsible for both the situation and the solution to our conundrum.

The pertinent question then seems to be, How do we help people educate themselves? This book has begun to answer that question. We've seen the stories of people who have learned without the structures of institutions, and I hope you can do the same. We've seen people who have learned to become independent critical thinkers, and I hope you can do the same. Ultimately that's what this debate is about: Do we trust young people to make their own decisions? Do we trust them to be curious?

I am not arguing against school, I am writing in favor of choices. You—we—must learn that we can make our own decisions. We can take data, evaluate them, and come up with a solution. We don't need our teachers to tell us the answer. We don't need our parents to give us hints. We, as individuals, have the power and capacity to make our own decisions. Hacking your education is a lifelong commitment. A lifelong commitment to forge your own path and define your own values. Not accepting what others want for you, but figuring it out for yourself.

That's scary enough. Scarier still is that most of us don't even have the freedom to figure those things out. Instead, we think everyone should be shipped off to school so they can get good grades, so that later they can be shipped off to college to do the same. The cycle continues. It's these expectations that I want to change with this book. I don't want college to disappear. No, I want college to become a question. I hope young people ask, Should I go to college? instead of, Where should I go to college?

Change is coming, though. Books like *Deschooling Society*, by Ivan Illich, who helped launch the unschooling philosophy, actually offer concrete proposals for how to apply advanced technology to solve educational problems. Particularly striking is the call in the book for the creation of "learning webs":

The operation of a peer-matching network would be simple. The user would identify himself by name and address and describe the activity for which he sought a peer. A computer would send him back the names and addresses of all those who had inserted the same description. It is amazing that such a simple utility has never been used on a broad scale for publicly valued activity.[3]

This was written in 1971, long before the Internet or even the idea of computer networking existed. But in 1971 we didn't have the technology to create some of the ideas Ivan Illich and others had; today we do.

The advancement of technology means that educational institutions are being dismantled. This is not something that will happen in five or ten years; it is happening right before our eyes. What's more amazing still is that universities and schools are starting to *dismantle themselves.*

In their place are rising companies, groups, and organizations that are replacing the different functions of the university. Instead of going to class, you can watch lectures online through the Khan Academy, OpenCourseWare, EdX, Udacity, or Coursera. You can form groups with your peers in the real world with tools like Open Study, Skillshare, and HourSchool. You can build online portfolios to prove your knowledge, gain badges from your learning, or be evaluated by new firms like Degreed, Smarterer, or Entelo that will help you get a job based on your knowledge. They couldn't care less where you went to school or whether you have a degree. They want to know what you can do.

And just like that, the three major functions of a university— knowledge delivery, community building, and employer signaling—

are replaced. The arbitrage has begun. As hackademics, we should welcome these changes as opportunities to become more responsible for our own education. The future, quite honestly, depends on it. I believe in you. I trust you. Together we can build a happy and healthy society. Enjoy the change. It's uncomfortable. That's how you know it's working.

Some schools are making changes to improve their pedagogy so they can stay competitive in a market where traditional universities are not the only players. Stanford, in part in response to the wild success of the massive open online courses (MOOCs), just appointed a dean of online learning. The first two MOOCs that Stanford ran, in fact, turned into Coursera and Udacity. But Stanford is not the only school that understands that the model is changing. Schools like Olin College, Philadelphia University, the Center for Research and Interdisciplinarity, and the Michael Polanyi College have all started programs that offer students the opportunity to engage in truly self-directed learning within a university setting. The future of the traditional college education is probably a powerful mix of online courses and the types of collaborative learning groups described in this book. It's so exciting to watch the revolution unfold before our eyes. The future is bright.

At UnCollege we're doing out part to advance the educational revolution. In 2013 we're launching the UnCollege Gap Year program to take ten of the smartest young people we find through the process of not going to college. We've created a curriculum of experiences (like finding mentors, teaching peer-to-peer classes, living in foreign countries, and so on) that this exclusive group will participate in.

There will be no taking English 101. We won't be telling anyone what to learn. Instead, we'll be facilitating a learning environment in which you can explore yourself and the world.

I encourage you to apply to the program at www.uncollege.org/gapyear.

ACKNOWLEDGMENTS

I want to start by thanking my parents, Lisa Nalbone and Pierre Stephens, who allowed me to leave school when I was twelve. None of this would have happened without them.

I owe great thanks to Rebecca Goldman and Demetri Sampas for providing the spark for the idea of UnCollege.org; to Patrick Mandia for patiently listening to my first UnCollege pitch; to Eric Lew for helping define the UnCollege vision; to Alice Floros for jumping on board to pitch conferences and competitions; to Hillel Levine for backing me up on my first news article; and to the students, faculty, and staff of Hendrix College for putting up with my efforts to undermine the collegiate system.

I want to thank Audrey Watters for asking for the first UnCollege interview; to Brandon Paton for being an early sounding board; to all my friends I constantly pestered about the idea; to Sandeep Paruchuri, Ricky Yean, Justin Leung, Daniela Lapidous, and Brian Wong for providing early feedback on the idea; and to Goran Kimogavoski for inviting me to speak at TEDxKidsBC when I was an unproven speaker.

I immensely appreciate Michael Ellsberg for working with me (someone he didn't know) to craft a book proposal; to Julien Smith for providing feedback and encouragement throughout the writing process; to Sandra Aamodt, Ryan Holiday, Suzanne Walsh, Dylan Field, Marlon Pain, Lisa Betts-La Croix, Astra Taylor, and Dave Hoover for providing excellent notes and feedback. Thank you to Sandra Aamodt for introducing me to my amazing agent, Lindsay Edgecombe, who worked tirelessly with me to help me understand what the hell I had agreed to do; to Tyler Driscoll for his amazing work on the cover; to Maria Gagliano for her fabulous editing; and to Justin Keenan for his editing expertise.

I love Mick Hagen for giving me that first job in Silicon Valley. You were right that I'd come back and wouldn't last at college.

I want to thank Peter Thiel and all the people at the Thiel Foundation—Jonathan Cain, Jim O'Neill, Danielle Strachman, Deepali Roy, and Mike Gibson—for supporting and challenging me as a Thiel Fellow.

Thank you to my close friends. Thank you to Elizabeth Stark for introducing me to more people than probably anyone else, and thank you to Rose Broome, for unconditionally loving and supporting me. Thank you to Scott Pheonix, Jo Pheonix, Natalie Warne, Todd Perry, David Dalrymple, Tyler Driscoll, Olof Mathe, and Sandra Aamodt for supporting me and loving me throughout this whole process. I love you all.

Thank you to Nicole Patrice Johnson for reminding me to be my authentic self. Thank you to Asha Jadeja for welcoming me as part of your family. Thank you to Kyle MacDonald for reminding me how ridiculous my life is. Thank you Bay McLaughlin for reminding me to give credit to others. Thank you to Jenny 8 Lee for directing me to helpful writing resources. Thank you to Henry Eyring for early feedback. Thank you to Cindy Gallop for reminding me to be myself. Thank you to Alex Peake for being awesome. Thank you to Sophie Denofrio for being my first friend at college. Thank you to Eden Full and Zac Bissonnette for calling my bullshit. Thank you to Max Weisel for always empathizing. Thank you to Roy Bahat for an amazing dinner. Thank you to Holly Epstein Ojalvo for writing about me at the *New York Times* and becoming a close friend. Thank you to Reihan Salam for asking interesting questions. Thank you to Greg Miller for helping me navigate TED. Thank you to all of the hackademic camp participants!

Thank you to the entire UnCollege.com team—Marlon Paine, Stef Grossano, Alex Berger, Kathryn Cannon, Joe Antenucci—none of this would be possible without you!

Thank you to Derrick Carter for showing me by example how to stay grounded despite flying about two hundred thousand miles in 2012. Thank you to everyone who has invited me to speak around the world and share the experience of self-directed learning.

ENDNOTES

Chapter 1: Understanding the System

1. Catherine Rampell, "Many with New College Degrees Find Job Market Humbling," *New York Times*, May 18, 2011, www.nytimes.com/2011/05/19/business/economy/19grads.html.

2. Richard Vedder, "Why Did 17 Million Students Go to College?," *Chronicle of Higher Education*, October 20, 2010, http://chronicle.com/blogs/innovations/why-did-17-million-students-go-to-college/27634.

3. Institute of Education Sciences, National Center for Education Statistics, "Fast Facts: Tuition Costs of Colleges and Universities," http://nces.ed.gov/fastfacts/display.asp?id=76.

4. Sandy Baum and Jennifer Ma, "Education Pays: The Benefits of Higher Education for Individuals and Society," Trends in Higher Education Series, 2007, www.collegeboard.com/prod_downloads/about/news_info/trends/ed_pays_2007.pdf.

5. Consumer Financial Protection Bureau, "Press Release: Consumer Financial Protection Bureau Releases Financial Aid Comparison Shopper," April 11, 2012, www.consumerfinance.gov/pressreleases/consumer-financial-protection-bureau-releases-financial-aid-comparison-shopper.

6. Richard Arum and Josipa Roska, *Academically Adrift: Limited Learning on College Campuses* (Chicago: University of Chicago Press, 2010).

7. Philip Babcock and Mindy Marks, "USA: The Decline in Student Study Time," www.econ.ucsb.edu/~babcock/LeisureCollege2.pdf.

8. National Center for Education Statistics, U.S. Department of Education, "Issue Brief: 1.5 Million Homeschooled Students in the United States in 2007," December 2008, http://nces.ed.gov/pubs2009/2009030.pdf.

9. Jeffrey R. Young, "Disgruntled College Student Starts UnCollege to Challenge System," February 9, 2011, http://chronicle.com/blogs/wiredcampus/disgruntled-college-student-starts-uncollege-to-challenge-system/29631.

Chapter 2: The Hackademic Mind-Set

1. Brian Ray, *Strengths of Their Own: Home Schoolers Across America* (Salem, OR: National Home Education Research Institute, 1997).

2. Brian Ray, "Research Facts on Homeschooling," January 11, 2011, www.nheri.org/research/research-facts-on-homeschooling.html.

3. National Center for Home Education, "Home Schoolers in Ivy League Universities," May 3, 2000, www.hslda.org/docs/nche/000002/00000234.asp.

4. M. A. Carskadon, A. R. Wolfson, C. Acebo, O. Tzischinsky, and R. Seifer, *Adolescent Sleep Patterns, Circadian Timing, and Sleepiness at a Transition to Early School Days* (Providence, RI: Sleep Research Laboratory, E. P. Bradley Hospital, 1998).

5. R. K. Biss and L. Hasher, "Happy as a Lark: Morning-Type Younger and Older Adults Are Higher in Positive Affect," *Emotion* 12, no. 3 (June 2012): 437–44.

6. Y. Shoda, W. Mischel, and P. Peak, "Predicting Adolescent Cognitive and Self-Regulatory Competencies from Preschool Delay of Gratification: Identifying Diagnostic Conditions," *Developmental Psychology* 20, no. 6 (1990): 978–86.

7. E. L. Deci, A. J. Schwartz, L. Sheinman, and R. M. Ryan, "An Instrument to Assess Adults' Orientations Toward Control Versus Autonomy with Children: Reflections on Intrinsic Motivation and Perceived Competence," *Journal of Educational Psychology* 73, no. 5 (1981): 642–50. R. M. Ryan and W. S. Grolnick, "Origins and Pawns in the Classroom: Self-Report and Projective Assessments of Individual Differences in Children's Perceptions," *Journal of Personality and Social Psychology* 50, no. 3 (1981): 550–58.

8. K. A. Renninger, "Individual Interest and Development: Implications for Theory and Practice," in *The Role of Interest in Learning and Development*, ed. K. A. Renninger, S. Hidi, and A. Krapp (Hillsdale, NJ: Lawrence Erlbaum, 1992), 381.

9. P. G. Anand and S. M. Ross, "Using Computer-Assisted Instruction to Personalize Arithmetic Materials for Elementary School Children," *Journal of Educational Psychology* 80, no. 3 (1987): 260–67.

10. M. R. Lepper, D. Greene, and R. E. Nisbett, "Undermining Children's Intrinsic Interest with Extrinsic Reward: A Test of the 'Overjustification' Hypothesis," *Journal of Personality and Social Psychology* 28, no. 1 (1973): 129–37.

11. E. L. Deci, "Effects of Externally Mediated Rewards on Intrinsic Motivation," *Journal of Personality and Social Psychology* 18, no. 1 (1971): 105–15.

12. Scott Belsky, *Making Ideas Happen* (New York: Penguin Group, 2010).

13. David Allen, *Getting Things Done* (New York: Penguin Books, 2002).

Chapter 3: Identifying Your Talents

1. C. S. Dweck, *Self-Theories: Their Role in Motivation, Personality, and Development* (Philadelphia: Psychology Press/Taylor & Francis, 1999).

2. B. L. Frederickson, "The Role of Positive Emotions in Positive Psychology: The Broaden-and-Build Theory of Positive Emotions," *American Psychologist* 56, no. 3 (2001): 218–26.

Chapter 4: Finding Mentors and Teachers

1. Eric Westervelt, "The Secret to Germany's Low Youth Unemployment," *Morning Edition* [NPR], April 14, 2012, www.npr.org/2012/04/04/149927290/the-secret-to-germanys-low-youth-unemployment.

2. Tucker Max, "How To: Find a Mentor (and Succeed Even If You Don't)," *Tuck erMax.Me*, April 16, 2012, http://tuckermax.me/how-to-find-a-mentor.

Chapter 5: Building a Community/Network

1. Jessica Dickler, "The Hidden Job Market," *CNN Money*, June 10, 2009, http://money.cnn.com/2009/06/09/news/economy/hidden_jobs/index.htm.

Chapter 7: Learning from the World

1. "Frequent-Flyer Miles: In Terminal Decline?," January 6, 2005, www.economist.com/node/3536178?story_id=E1_PVPGTSR.

Epilogue: Education Hacking Is Lifelong

1. Richard Arum and Josipa Roksa, *Academically Adrift: Limited Learning on College Campuses* (Chicago: University of Chicago Press, 2010).

2. W. C. Symonds, R. Schwartz, and R. F. Ferguson, *Pathways to Prosperity: Meeting the Challenge of Preparing Young Americans for the 21st Century* (Cambridge: Pathways to Prosperity Project, Harvard University Graduate School of Education, 2011).

3. Ivan Illich, *Deschooling Society* (New York: Harper & Row, 1971).